D0149413

THE *Sea* IS SO *Wide*

AND MY *Boat* IS SO *Small*

THE *Sea* IS SO *Wide*
AND MY *Boat* IS SO *Small*

CHARTING *a* COURSE *for the* NEXT GENERATION

Marian Wright Edelman

HYPERION

NEW YORK

Author's Note

Unless otherwise indicated, the prayers in this book are the work of the author.

CDF Freedom Schools® and Cradle to Prison Pipeline® are both registered trademarks of the Children's Defense Fund.

"Greenless Child" by Ann Weems. From Reaching for Rainbows. Copyright © 1980 Anne Barr Weems. Used by permission of Westminster John Knox Press.

Library of Congress Cataloging-in-Publication Data

Edelman, Marian Wright.
    The sea is so wide and my boat is so small : charting a course for the next generation / Marian Wright Edelman.
        p.   cm.
    ISBN 978-1-4013-2333-2
    1. Child rearing—United States.   2. Children—United States—Conduct of life.   3. African American children—Conduct of life.   4. United States—Moral conditions.   I. Title.
HQ769.E3554 2008
179'.20973—dc22

2008026521

Hyperion books are available for special promotions, premiums, or corporate training. For details contact Michael Rentas, Proprietary Markets, Hyperion, 77 West 66th Street, 12th floor, New York, New York 10023, or call 212-456-0133.

Design by Susan Walsh

FIRST EDITION

10 9 8 7 6 5 4 3 2 1

This book is dedicated to the legacy of my parents,
Arthur Jerome Wright and Maggie Leola Wright,
and to all their children's children: Joshua, Jonah, and Ezra
Julian Jr., Stan, Stephanie, and Crystal
Debbie, Harryeta, Harry Jr., and Schwannah
Pandit, Arthur Jr., and Carolyn
Joy and Maggie
and their children.

To my beloved grandchildren, Ellika,
Zoe, Elijah, and Levi
and all to come.
And to Peyton, Sixiu, and Michael.

It is also dedicated to all the children with whom they
must share the world and to those who work tirelessly to build
a future fit and safe for every child.

Finally, this book is dedicated to the legacy of Martin Luther King Jr.
and Robert Francis Kennedy with faith and hope that their last
campaign in 1968 to end poverty in America will
become reality in our lifetime.

Contents

Acknowledgments

I am deeply grateful to my cheerful and always helpful special assistant Michele Smith who worked tirelessly to help me complete this book; to CDF colleagues Karen Lashman, Janet Simons, Catherine Crato, Maria Aguirre, Lisa Robinson, and Susan Gates for their policy and research support; to Deanne Urmy who cast a helpful eye on an early draft; to Shannon Daley-Harris for review of the faith leaders chapter; and to Julia Cass who reported on the Wake County, North Carolina, School System.

Deepest thanks to dear friends Guido Goldman, Deborah Szekely, Laura Chasin, and Carol Biondi for their warm hospitality and sharing of beautiful and quiet spaces to write; to CDF board member Katie McGrath and friends Richard Lovett and Michelle Kydd Lee who encouraged this book. Thanks, too, to Robert Miller for his support and to Gretchen Young, my fine editor.

I am so thankful for the lives of Gordon and Mary Cosby of the Church of the Saviour Ministries and of Dr. and Mrs. Eliott "Mom and Dad" Mason for their continuing prayers, friendship, spiritual support, and personification of what it means to be a person of faith.

Foreword

*God, we have pushed so many of our children into the tumultuous sea of life
in small and leaky boats without survival gear and compass.*
Forgive us and help them to forgive us.
*Help us now to give all our children the anchors of faith and love, the rudders
of purpose and hope, the sails of health and education, and the paddles of
family and community*
to keep them safe and strong when life's sea gets rough.

As my firstborn son Joshua approached his twenty-first birthday
and graduation from college, I thought for many months about
what I could give him and his younger brothers Jonah and Ezra
as they crossed the threshold of adulthood. So I decided to write
them a letter that evolved into a book, *The Measure of Our Success: A
Letter to My Children and Yours.* It was a spiritual and family dowry,
with some of the important values my parents and community
elders and ancestors believed in and struggled to live by, and
which shaped my life. I also shared some of the lessons that life
had taught me, which my sons could use or ignore as they chose.

Since then I have been blessed with four beautiful grand-children who have touched my deepest heartstrings and evoked a renewed sense of responsibility. I look at our nation and world with heightened alertness for beauty and joy to share, and for dangers that may threaten these dearest gifts, and I ask: What kind of families, communities, nation, and world are we adults passing on to our children and grandchildren? What values are we instilling by our actions as parents, grandparents, faith leaders, educators, and political, community, and cultural leaders and citizens? What legacies are we bequeathing through the moral and economic choices we are making today? Are their nation and world safer or more dangerous? Will their standard of living and quality of life be better or worse than ours? Will our children and grandchildren be able to afford and get the quality of education needed to compete and contribute in an ever more demanding and rapidly changing, globalizing world? Will our nation be able to bridge and close our huge divides of race, income, and gender to foster respect and justice for all people?

In this first decade of a new century, our nation and world have veered alarmingly offtrack, become less safe, less just, more precarious and balkanized. The gap between rich and poor in the United States and the world are the highest ever recorded. A cloud of nuclear annihilation hangs over every child and human being. Global warming threatens our mother earth. Before and after 9/11, we have come too slowly to recognize the oneness of our porous world where disease, pollution, climate change, and terrorism know no borders and require collaborative solutions. And the militarism, the excessive materialism, the racism, and the poverty Dr. Martin Luther King Jr. warned could lead to our national and global destruction still run rampant.

Violence stalks children and all of us everywhere—in schools, universities, shopping malls, and on the streets. The pollution of our air, water, food, and earth, and the coarsening discourse on our airwaves, Internet, and media leave virtually no child untouched. Moral, community, and family values have frayed and millions of children in all race and income groups are growing up without hope or a sense of moral purpose. Adult hypocrisy in too many homes, schools, communities, religious institutions, and private and public sector policies is confusing and leading many children astray as they do what we do rather than what we say. It is time for us adults to get our act together and stop dropping the ball of responsibility for our children's well-being and future. In the United States, we have a child and youth problem because we have a profound adult problem.

Children need positive and authentic adult role models as well as voices challenging our cultural addictions to power, money, celebrity, violence, alcohol, drugs, as well as obsessive materialism and individualism. They need to see leaders developing a concept of enough for all, and fairer policies, as the rich get richer as children get poorer. They need adults to teach them how to struggle with complexity; to think through the short- and long-term consequences of their actions; to bounce back from life's inevitable failures; to learn how not to be lonely when alone; to think, ask the right questions, solve problems, sort out and synthesize reams of information, make informed judgments, and take effective action; to sacrifice to build a fairer and safer world; and to listen for the genuine which according to the gospels and prophets of every great faith dwells within each of us.

While thirteen million underprivileged children in the richest nation on earth are growing up in indefensible poverty without the most basic necessities of life and a fair chance to envisage a better future, millions of overprivileged children are growing up infected with the affluenza virus—the spiritual poverty of having too much that is worth too little. Given every material thing they desire—cell phones, iPods, fancy cars, and the latest trendy fashions—while living in big houses in well-to-do neighborhoods, many lack sufficient parental and community attention, limit-setting, spiritual guidance, and moral example. They roam around in peer herds from one place to another trying out drugs, alcohol, tobacco, loveless sex, and race- and gay-bashing, seeking entertainment and thrills with increasingly high thresholds for the bizarre and violent just like many of the children left behind in the ghettos and barrios. These lost, out of control children are desperately crying out for attention, direction, and protection from parents and other responsible adults.

I don't want my grandchildren, or any child, growing up in a rich nation that thinks it can imprison its way out of the glaring inequities in our society and suck poor children of color into a pipeline to prison. I don't want them growing up with leaders infected with a sense of entitlement who think we can bully our way to world leadership through hubris and military might rather than moral right. I don't want them growing up in a nation that continues to marginalize and mistreat millions of children and people of all ages because of their color, income, disability, gender, faith, or ethnicity. I don't want them growing up in a country that gives lip service to equal opportunity while neglecting the poor, the sick, the orphan, and the stranger our faith traditions enjoin us to help. I do not want them growing up in a culture that objectifies and degrades any of our daughters and where any of our sons believe that manhood comes from seeking superiority over women and that fatherhood ends with conception. And I don't want them growing up believing that profits are more important than people, missiles are more important than mothers, bombs are more valuable than babies, sacrifice is a dirty word, and nonviolence is for softies.

Although I share many sobering realities in the letters here, this book is not about doom-and-gloom. It is about waking up, getting off your duff, and standing up and reclaiming our children, families, communities, our moral values, and our nation. It is a call to conscience and to action for all who seek to build and leave the world we hold in trust for the next generations better than we found it. It is an appeal to all those who are eager to be beacons of hope and who have faith, like Indian philosopher Rabindranath Tagore's "bird that feels the light and sings when the dawn is still dark."

I *know* we can transform our nation and world because we have seen the impossible happen in our lifetime: the crumbling of the centuries-old walls of legal racial apartheid in America thanks to the courageous witness of a small minority of parents, children, and lawyers who wanted a decent education and better life for black children and thanks to the countless black and white citizens who built a Civil Rights Movement to end legal segregation in American life. We've seen the fall of the Berlin Wall, symbolizing the end of the Cold War and the breakup of the Soviet Union and Communism across Eastern Europe. And we watched in awe as Nelson Mandela walked out of prison ramrod straight after twenty-seven years, extending a hand of reconciliation to his former jailers.

You and I now have the opportunity—and awesome responsibility—to compose and play the next movement of America's symphony of freedom and justice—to forge a nation where more good people outplan and outmobilize evil people; where more people fight for justice than those who fight to maintain an unjust status quo; where more people committed to nonviolence outorganize and challenge those who saturate our nation with guns and destabilize or destroy our nations with war. Together we can build a nation that will be able to pass the test of the God of history asking whether we gave food to the hungry and clothes to the naked, cared for the sick, visited those in prison, gave water to the thirsty, and saw and helped the least of these my children.

Seventy-nine years ago a black baby named Martin Luther King Jr. was born in America. He grew up to become our greatest twentieth-century American prophet. In 1968—forty years ago—he was killed as he called on us to end our warring and greedy ways, the poverty staining our wealthy land, and to confront the triple evils of militarism, materialism, and racism that would lead to our destruction. Rabbi Abraham Joshua Heschel believed "the whole future of America depended on his impact and influence." I agree and wanted to write letters to him, our leaders, and us citizens reporting on our progress and what remains to be done.

2008 has been a time of great hope as our nation strives to move beyond race and gender, but it has also been a time of great challenge as growing incarceration and a cradle-to-prison pipeline fueled by epidemic poverty and continuing racial disparities threaten to usher in a new era of American apartheid for millions of children and youth left behind, unless we act together with urgency to reroute all our children to productive adulthood. We have a momentous choice as to whether we will repeat the mistakes of the past or move forward to realize Dr. King's and America's dream.

There are letters to parents, teachers and educators, neighbors and community leaders, and to women—especially mothers and grandmothers. While parents have primary responsibility to care for children, nobody raises a child alone, and parents need the support of caring communities. And I believe that if we are going to have fundamental paradigm change, women, the bearers of life, will have to demand it.

Finally, I write letters to young people with some life lessons they can take or leave and to my beloved grandchildren with my hopes and wishes for them and for all grandchildren to come and their children and grandchildren. The last letter asks God's guidance and help to create in us the spiritual and political will to end poverty and racism and war and to raise high the torch of freedom and justice in a world desperately hungering for hope and peace.

THE *Sea* IS SO *Wide*

AND MY *Boat* IS SO *Small*

A Letter to Parents

A PRAYER FOR TWENTY-FIRST-CENTURY CHILDREN

God, help us to not raise a new generation of children
With high intellectual quotients and low caring and compassion quotients
With sharp competitive edges but dull cooperative instincts
With highly developed computer skills but poorly developed consciences
With a gigantic commitment to the big "I" but little sense of responsibility
*   to the bigger "we"*
With mounds of disconnected and unsynthesized information without a moral
*   context to determine its worth*
With more and more knowledge and less and less imagination and appreciation
*   for the magic of life that cannot be quantified or computerized*
With more and more worldliness and less and less wonder and awe for the sacred
*   and everyday miracles of life.*
God, help us to raise children who care.

It's not good enough for you to say to your child, "Do good in school"; and
then when the child comes home, you've got the TV set on. You've got the
radio on. You don't check their homework. You've got the video game
playing. . . . So turn off the TV set. Put the video games away. Buy a little
desk. Or put that child at the kitchen table. Watch them do their homework.
If they don't know how to do it, give 'em help. If you don't know how to do
it, call the teacher. Make 'em go to bed at a reasonable time! Keep 'em off the
streets! Give 'em some breakfast! . . . And if your child misbehaves in school,
don't cuss out the teacher! Do something with your child!

—SENATOR BARACK OBAMA, SPEAKING TO A
BEAUMONT, TEXAS, AUDIENCE, FEBRUARY 28, 2008
(*LOS ANGELES TIMES,* FEBRUARY 29, 2008)

*P*arenting is the most wonderful and daunting challenge in the
world, never to be undertaken lightly. No one should have a
child if they are not committed to providing love, attention,
protection, care, and support for a lifetime. Although families
are the crucible of the future and the primary molders of children's values, parenting is one of the most undervalued and least
prepared for roles in America. The nation and world are literally
being born anew every second of every day in the bodies and
minds and spirits of each baby entrusted to the adults who bear
primary responsibility for their safety and nurturance.

Parents are children's most important teachers and mentors,
but many of us, especially if we are teens or poor or lacked a
stable family life ourselves, need guidance and help. Virtually all
parents want to be good parents but some do not know how and
many lack a network of support. Nobody raises a child alone.
Too often parents are judged and blamed rather than helped
to meet their children's needs in a society where family life has
been atomized; extended family, community bonds, and moral

boundaries have frayed; and private sector and government policies often make it harder rather than easier for parents to meet their children's needs.

Parenting has become more and more difficult in our dazzlingly fast-paced world mired down in materialism, violence, fame, celebrity worship, and triviality. With technology's instant and massive reach, the relentless virus of commercial and entertainment messaging to children at earlier and earlier ages is difficult to avoid, forcing parents to compete with powerful outside cultural forces for children's attention and values. Childhood innocence, play, and imagination are being intruded upon more and more by profiteers seeking new markets and trying to addict parents through their children to their brands. Many parents are pressured into buying the latest designer sneakers and jeans and other "stuff" they cannot afford, working more hours to satisfy children who seek to keep up with peers and spending less time at home. In our increasingly coarse and profane public marketplace, mutual respect and any sense of the sacred has eroded, extrinsic values are glorified over intrinsic ones, making it difficult to guide children toward more authentic and purposeful lives. Buying is equated with happiness. Money and fame are equated with success. Children are not just sold products but sex, alcohol, tobacco, and violence as the way to be accepted and hip.

At its 350th anniversary, Harvard reported the top three goals of its entering freshmen as (1) money, (2) power, and (3) reputation and fame. Are these the values we truly want our children to treasure? Will the pursuit of such individualistic goals bring our nation and world closer together or drive us further apart? Are these the measures of success we want to leave our children as parents, people of faith, and citizens of a great democracy in a globalizing world desperately hungering for moral leadership? If money, power, and personal fame are the central values in our lives, then human values and fair sharing with those left behind get lost. Children are treated as consumers, market values trump moral values, and personal greed trumps common good. I believe the prophets and the Gospels, history, and common sense beckon us as parents, grandparents, and adults today to reassess what we are to live by, teach our children and struggle harder to model.

How can parents today better educate children about our deepest human challenges and give them the moral compasses and skills they need to navigate life, cyberspace, and a globalizing world driven largely by market forces? How can we buffer our children against the dangerous undertow of alcohol, drugs, violence, and excessive consumption that often capsize their boats? Can parents, teachers, faith leaders, and communities offer more strenuous competition to these threats with more love, family time, and community engagement? How do we prepare our children to respect and live in peace with people of many cultures, languages, faiths, ideologies, and colors in a world that is majority nonwhite and poor and in our own nation, which will be majority minority around 2050?

So many of our children are struggling to cope with family breakdown from pervasive divorce and the added stresses many single-parent families face: babies born to unmarried mothers constitute more than one third of all and more than two thirds of black births. All children suffer from the erosion of extended family and community supports, the loss of civility evidenced by road rage, profane language, and ever coarsening public discourse so common in our culture. Epidemic substance abuse, domestic violence, and mental illness know no income boundaries.

I am often asked, What's wrong with our children? Children

having children. Children killing children. Children killing
themselves. Children roaming streets alone or in gangs all day
and night. Children floating through life like driftwood on a
beach. Children addicted to tobacco, alcohol, heroin, cocaine,
pot, drinking and drugging themselves to death to escape reality. Children running away from home and being thrown away
or abused and neglected by parents. Children being locked up in
jails with adult criminal mentors or all alone. Children bubbling
with rage and crushed by depression.

Adults are what's wrong with our children. Parents letting
children raise themselves or be raised by television or the Internet. Children being shaped by peers and gangs instead of parents, grandparents, and kin. Children roaming the streets because
there's nobody at home or paying enough attention. Children
going to drug houses that are always open instead of to schools
and church houses, mosques, and temples that are too often
closed. Children seeing adults take and sell drugs and be violent
to one another and to them. Adults telling children one thing
and doing another. Adults making promises we don't keep and
preaching what we don't practice. Adults telling children to control themselves while slapping and spanking. Adults telling children to be honest while lying and cheating in our homes, offices,
and public life. Adults telling children not to be violent while
marketing and glorifying violence and tolerating gun-saturated
communities. Adults telling children to be healthy and wondering why they are obese while selling them junk food. Adults are
what's wrong with our children and I hope God will help us to
repent.

It is time for parents, adults, and leaders in all race and income groups to break our silence about the pervasive breakdown
of moral, family, community, and national values; to place our

children first in our lives and struggle harder to model the behavior we want our children to learn. We do not have a child and youth problem in the United States but we have a *profound* adult problem as our children do what they see adults doing. Children seek our attention in negative ways when we provide them too few positive ways to communicate and to get the attention and love they need.

All children need hope, a stable family, a sense of connectedness to a community, engagement in something beyond self, positive alternatives to the streets, and inner compasses to help them resist negative cultural and street lures. All children need imperishable spiritual anchors rather than fleeting material ones and the regular presence of and interaction with positive and consistent adult mentors to move beyond obsessive self-gratification. All children need adults to put their needs first and buffer them from harmful external assaults.

My daddy and mama always put me, my sister, and brothers first. They did not have much money but they had a lot of love and high expectations for each of us. The external world told me, a black girl growing up in the racially segregated South, that I wasn't as valuable as little white children but I didn't believe it because my parents said it wasn't so. The outside world put a lot of obstacles in my way, including segregated public accommodations and libraries and unequally funded schools, but my parents valued education and made sure we always had books in our home. My parents could not buy us a lot of clothes but they taught us how to take care of the ones we had, passed them down from child to child, and paid no attention to the latest fads and fashions, which was far easier before television and the Internet. We had few luxuries but all we needed to get to school on time and be able to learn: a hot breakfast and dinner waiting after school; a time, place, and help for homework; an established playtime, bath time, and bedtime—structured routines that made us feel safe and valued. Lying and profanity were not tolerated and laziness was not an option. We had daily chores at home and on the weekends in the church and community: setting the table; washing and drying the dishes; cleaning the house, our clothes, and the yard; and taking out the garbage. No excuses were allowed. Daddy picked up and made us pick up litter without regard for who put it there, saying if your street is dirty, that is no reason for your house, yard, or room to be.

My parents sacrificed for us—all the time. If our growing feet needed new shoes, they wore old ones. They believed in lifelong learning and growth, attending conferences, and subscribing to publications to improve themselves. Above all, they believed in holding family together through thick and thin. I am astonished rereading some of Daddy's sermons by his emphasis on parental duty in maintaining a stable home for children amid change and his recognition of the impact of external forces on children. So many today point to families as the sole source of children's problems, ignoring how economic and social changes affect child and family well-being. When plants close and jobs move abroad, families and children are hurt.

The security and discipline of family life guided my childhood years and grounds me still. While I have been a far from perfect parent, I've struggled to carry on as many of those traditional routines as possible and to share with my wonderful sons and grandchildren what is important and expected as my parents and elders did with me. So for all beleaguered and devoted parents today, I share a bill of responsibilities learned in childhood that may be of use in steering children to safe harbor.

A PARENT'S BILL OF RESPONSIBILITIES

Make sure your children know they are loved unconditionally and forever and ever and that nothing they do can ever take away your or God's love. Children need to be loved for *who* they are and not just for how much they achieve or how they look or for any external reason. Although all parents want children to do well in school and are proud of talents they possess, it is important that children know that they are valued because they simply are—God's sacred child and your special child.

Know where your children are and make sure they know where you are! "One of the oldest human needs is having someone to wonder where you are when you don't come home at night," anthropologist Margaret Mead said. When I was young, my family had a practice of calling when any of us arrived at a destination so we all knew we were safe. This is very reassuring, although some adult children may think this practice intrusive. It's about caring. How traumatic it is for a child or young person to have parents disappear for hours, days, months, or forever without knowing why or where we are. Leave a note. Call. Better still, try not to leave children for any significant period without patiently explaining the reason.

Be a good role model and mentor for your children. You are the most important person in your children's lives and they take their cues from you about what is right and wrong and valuable. If we call our children and others disrespectful names, they will do so too. If we tell jokes that demean people of other races or faiths or genders or with disabilities, they will too. If we abuse alcohol and drugs, they will too. If we are violent, they will think it acceptable. If we spend every dime on ourselves or on material things and give nothing or little to those less fortunate, they will follow our lead. If we spend hours watching TV, playing video games, listening to the radio, gossiping on the phone, and never pick up a book to read, they'll do the same. If we use profanity as a second language, they will too. Be mindful that we are always being watched. Author James Baldwin wrote that children seldom do what we tell them to do but they almost always do what we do. What an awesome responsibility we parents carry!

Don't tear down children's confidence—build it up. Applaud them when they do well. Don't tell children to "shut up," "sit down," or "stop asking all those questions," or "I'll smack you." I have sometimes heard mothers tell their little boys "you're not gonna amount to nothing just like your no-good daddy." They didn't choose their daddy, you did. Choose carefully and teach them to respect both parents. Do not involve your children in your adult fights that they did not cause. Reach out to uncles, grandfathers, and other positive male role models in your community so that girls and boys can forge safe and healthy relationships with men as well as women.

Really pay attention to each of your children. Many of us are so harried trying to cope with the demands of life and to juggle competing and often stressful demands of job and family that we sometimes forget to truly hear and appreciate our children. I think back with great regret to the times I was so busy getting things done at home or at work that I didn't just stop to be with and enjoy my sons and experience the world through their eyes and ears. Time *does* fly, as the old folks used to say, and children grow up in a blink of the eye. I would give anything to be able to recapture moments and occasions I missed or failed to savor with each child. With my grandchildren I hope I'll be much more relaxed, wiser, and able to spend special time with *each* child. This is hard in large families or when huge distances separate us across generations. In a recent telephone conversation with my four-year-old granddaughter, Zoe, she asked me where I was. I told her where I was traveling and that I had just sent her a postcard. She immediately asked whether I sent one just to her or to her *and* her sister Ellika. I sheepishly admitted that I had sent one to both of them, as I had to my twin grandsons, Elijah and Levi. But I went immediately to buy four others so that she and her sister and each twin could have one of their very own. I'll remember to do this from now on. I tried to send weekly postcards to each of my children, who sometimes complained that they could not read my terrible writing and figure out what I said. That's okay. They simply said, however illegibly, I love you and am thinking about you.

Don't think it's anybody else's responsibility to teach your children values, respect, and good manners. It's yours. *Thank you* and *please* are three of the most important words in the world. They can open or close many doors for your children. Practice them every day at home. Teach your children how to stand and sit up straight, to look people in the eye when they speak, to speak clearly and politely, to say "yes ma'am" and "sir" to older people, to say "I'm sorry" when they have erred, and not to call older adults by their first names. And teach them to dress sensibly and appropriately without pants hanging way too low and dresses hanging way too high.

Do not abuse tobacco, alcohol, cocaine, or other drugs that threaten your health and your ability to parent and that teach children harmful habits. And do not let people in your house or expose your children to people outside of your house who do. Try to avoid too many fast-food restaurant meals, which are contributing to childhood obesity and other health ills. A black woman organic farmer told me her Mississippi grandmother discouraged her from eating fast food because "there's no love in that food."

Establish and practice family rituals and provide as much consistency and structure in your children's home life as possible. Sit down for meals together whenever possible. Get up in the morning and get your children breakfast before they go to school. I cannot make it through the day without breakfast, which I consider the most important meal of the day, and I made sure my children began every day with a hot breakfast. (As some parents cannot or will not do this, it is important that schools utilize all existing breakfast, lunch, and summer feeding programs to ensure children are well fed and able to pay attention in school.) Set times for homework and make sure it's done before you permit children to do less important things like watching TV or chatting on the phone. Having a quiet space where children can do homework and read may be difficult or impossible for many poor families in crowded shared housing or homeless shelters, so schools, churches, and community centers must step into the gap. Encourage older siblings to help younger siblings with schoolwork and if you are working one, two, or more jobs, try to find an after-school program where your children can go until you come home. Set aside time for reading, play, and family outings. Set regular bath and bedtimes so children aren't exhausted the next day.

Don't let TV or the Internet raise your child. Cut off, limit, and monitor their TV and computer use. Don't let gangsta rappers raise your child. Do not put TVs or computers in children's rooms but in shared family spaces where you can see and discuss what is being watched. Try to help children engage in regular physical activities. Recreation at school and in safe supervised public playgrounds is important but increasingly scarce or unsafe in many poor neighborhoods.

Don't try to be your children's buddy or friend. Be their parent. Parenting is not a popularity contest or a feel-good-all-the-time occupation. Set limits and try to stick by them firmly and consistently. It is not an undertaking for the fainthearted. Parents should talk to each other and make sure they are conveying similar messages and rules.

Read to your child and encourage them to read even if you can't. Famed Johns Hopkins surgeon Ben Carson's mother was not well educated but she valued education. She took her sons to the library to get books and asked them to tell her about them.

Neither was Dr. James Comer's mother, but she raised a distinguished child psychiatrist son, a professor at the Yale Child Study Center and the creator of the Comer Process, a reform model to foster high achievement among poor children in inner city schools.

Don't let peers or strangers raise your children. Keep your children off the streets. This is hard for parents in many inner cities and rural areas who are working outside the home without neighborhood programs for children to attend after school, on weekends, and during long, idle summer months. This is where communities and public policies have to step up to the plate to help overstressed parents and see that children are safe and positively engaged.

Teach your children to work diligently, to focus, to persevere, and to complete the task at hand. Help them set goals and work toward them until they succeed. Too many young people today want to start at the top without walking up the stairs or stopping on the elevator at each floor. Most successful people have put in a lot of hard work over time and most big changes come from many small ones that add up to bigger changes over time.

Have high standards and expectations for your children and insist that schools do the same. Encourage and applaud their achievements. Get to know their teachers. Teach them to respect their teachers. Try to attend as many parent-teacher conferences and school programs as possible. Children need to feel your support. And schools need to see parents as partners in children's learning and make parents feel welcome and respected. Ask that teacher-parent conferences be scheduled at times as convenient as possible if you are working parents.

Don't do for your children what they can do for themselves or feel you have to be their full-time social secretary. It's okay for them to say "I'm bored." I used to call it daydreaming and I loved the hours and hours to myself when I could fantasize about all the things I would do and be and see when I grew up. Too many children in today's fast-paced, always-must-be-doing-something climate seek constant entertainment or motion, and are unable to pause and take time out just to be rather than be done to and for. Keep good books around for them to pick up.

Teach your children that they are powerful and can and must make a difference. Take them with you to vote, to community meetings and school board meetings, and to hear effective and visionary people speak and perform. My daddy used to drive us long distances to expose us to important leaders like Mary McLeod Bethune and Marian Anderson. Let them see you as an active participant—not just a talker and taker—in your community and civic life. And they can be more environmentally conscious in small and large ways beginning with recycling. My children and grandchildren were my environmental leaders.

Spend as much or more time and care on developing your children's character as on their intellect. Character and integrity are who we are when nobody else is looking. They are the compasses that steer us when we encounter rough times and that enable us to discern the genuine voices among a cacophony of false prophets.

Try to get to know the parents of your children's friends and watch the company your children keep. This is often very hard with teens. Always ask if the parents are going to be home when they request permission to go to parties and whether alcohol is to be served. This often made for uncomfortable discussions in my house but making the effort is important. Whether or not they appreciate it at the time, it says I care. My biggest challenges were with beach weeks as they got older where I knew drinking and other things were likely and adult supervision would be missing. My children hated my strictness and fearfulness but I was trying to do my job. It is a parent's job to set limits and teens' jobs to test them.

Don't condone, tell, snicker, or wink at racial, gender, religious, or ethnic jokes. Outlaw the hurtful N, B, and H words in your home that have gotten out of hand in our society. They sow division and disrespect. Teach your daughters not to answer to names you did not give them and teach your sons to use them at their peril. Teach both to respect themselves and others. We must make all actions—subtle or blatant—to demean another unacceptable in our presence and on our airwaves. Speak out against them. Stop patronizing advertisers and performers and companies that sponsor smut and intolerance.

Value and educate our sons and daughters equally since both will raise our grandsons and granddaughters. Let's stop spoiling and pampering our boys and raising our daughters. Boys need to be taught to clean up their own messes and to put down the toilet seat for the other half of humanity. And fathers and mothers must teach our boys and girls by example how to build healthy relationships and not let the media and Internet set our relationship standards at subbasement levels.

Give children regular chores so that they can learn how to share in meeting family needs and take responsibility for themselves and others. Children want to be helpful. I love how often my seven-year-old granddaughter, Ellika, asks me "Can I help you?" when I'm watering the plants or fixing dinner.

Say you're sorry when you say and do the wrong thing. Ask them to forgive you just as you forgive them when they make a mistake. Children don't expect us to be perfect but they expect us to admit when we do wrong. And all of us parents do.

Support the children you bring into the world as a mother or a father with love, attention, time, discipline, money, and good values. If you are not prepared to do this, please do not have children—and that means men and women. Becoming a parent should not be an accidental aside of a pleasure moment, a personal need for self-assurance, or an effort to keep a failing relationship alive. Children need fathers and mothers.

Be grateful for your children. They are God's most precious gifts and our messengers to the future.

ROLE MODEL

Parent, grandparent, aunt, uncle
Children are watching you today

What will they learn?

Teacher, preacher, president, governor, mayor
A child is depending on you
How will you repay their trust?

Coach, celebrity, citizen, neighbor
A child is emulating you today
What kind of human being will they become?

A Letter to Teachers and Educators

Teaching children may be the highest way to seek God. It is, however, also the most daunting way, in the sense of the greatest responsibility.

—GABRIELA MISTRAL, CHILEAN NOBEL PRIZE LAUREATE IN
LITERATURE

"I am a young African American teacher who came from a public school education, from an urban environment. My mom made less than $30,000 a year, and she raised me and four brothers. Now I'm in a position to empower all these people to have the same path that I was on." She tells her students they should not be afraid to go anywhere—to Japan (where she went on fellowship during college), or Africa, or India, or Antarctica. *"They ask me, 'If they send you to the moon, will you go?'"* she said. *"I say: 'Absolutely. You have to go everywhere. Life is bigger than Harlem.'"*

—*NEW YORK TIMES* ARTICLE ABOUT TWENTY-NINE-YEAR-OLD
HARLEM CHILDREN'S ZONE SCIENCE TEACHER MS. SHAKIRA
BROWN, WHO HAS VOLUNTEERED TO SPEND TWO MONTHS
IN ANTARCTICA ON A NATIONAL SCIENCE FOUNDATION
EXPEDITION

After parents, you are probably the greatest influencers and molders of children's futures. I recognize, though, the fierce competition educators and parents face from our cultural rogues—TV, movies, negative hip-hop and gangsta rap, video games, the Internet, and peers—that increasingly are displacing too many parents and educators as the primary molders of children's values.

Teachers are not sufficiently valued in our society if we measure your worth by America's highest value: money. Our society says you are over three hundred times less valuable than a corporate CEO of one of the five hundred largest companies whose average compensation was $15.2 million in 2006 compared to an elementary school teacher's average salary of $48,700. A high school teacher, however skilled and hardworking, earned less in a year ($51,150) than the $21 million one basketball star earned in one day, and 1,954 times less than the $100 million one golfer earned from advertisements in one year.

For many teachers and educators, I know it is not money that keeps you in the profession but I also know that better salaries would enable many more qualified people to enter and remain in it. We must do much more to recognize the importance of teaching in our nation and celebrate the best among you in a very visible way.

Teaching has to be more than just a job; it has to be a calling. I share Nobel Laureate in Literature and teacher Gabriela Mistral's belief that "a love for children opens up more paths for teachers than pedagogic theory does." You can have the best equipped school, smallest class size, and a great curriculum, but if teachers and principals do not love children, children will know it—and be hurt. So if you do not love children—all children—*please* get out of the classroom. If you do not respect and expect *all* children to learn, *please* find another job. If you do not believe all children are sacred, you do not belong in a school or in any child-serving agency. And if you are not excited about learning and committed to working hard to keep up, grow, and prepare continuously to make your lessons stimulating for children, you are in the wrong profession.

Teachers must be committed to finding and nourishing the gifts in each child and to building a child's sense of confidence and competence. Paulo Freire, respected Brazilian educator and author of *Pedagogy of the Oppressed,* also thought teachers have a duty to reflect constant commitment to justice in relationships with students. If you cannot be fair to each child, you will do harm.

A child's self-esteem is often fragile, especially if that child lacks crucial family encouragement as so many do. Teachers' negative attitudes and messages can compound a child's learning difficulties but a teacher's regular compliments and support can motivate, and even save a child's life. Children need adults who never give up on them, are constantly searching for their special gifts, and who refuse to let them fail. If you see a child with special needs that are not being met, call it to the attention of someone who can help. If you do not advocate for children whose parents cannot or do not, who else will?

Every child who is not taught to read and compute in school is being sentenced to social and economic death in our globalizing economy. He or she will be unable to fully perform the ordinary tasks of life; get a decent-paying job; or become a self-sufficient family member, an informed citizen, or a parent able to read to and interact with his or her children as many more educated parents can. While there are some very gifted uneducated parents who raise well-educated children, their struggle to meet their children's learning needs is harder. The cycle of poor education must be broken and you are responsible for breaking it with the support of parents and community leaders.

Much controversy swirls around testing and the No Child Left Behind Act, which diverts attention away from addressing the needs of the whole child. All tests are not bad, depending on their purpose and how they are used. If tests are not age validated and developmentally appropriate (as they are not for preschool children) they should not be used. If tests seek to assess students' skill level and proficiency so that schools can better meet the *individual* needs of individual children, then they are good *if* children's needs are met. If tests are just one and not the only measure for assessing a child's abilities and strengths and are not used to rigidly classify or misclassify children, then they can perform a useful function. If the excitement about teaching, learning, and thinking out of the box is not extinguished and teaching to the test does not become the single-minded focus of schools, then tests can play a useful role in assuring teacher accountability for educating children.

Children *must* achieve and those entrusted with educating them *must* perform. It is a national scandal and child catastrophe that our public schools are failing to provide millions of children, especially minority and poor children, skills they need to function in life. Consider these horrific numbers: Two thirds of *all* American public school fourth graders and 70 percent of *all* public school eighth graders cannot read at grade level. Only 12 percent of black, 14 percent of Hispanic, and 19 percent of Native American public school eighth graders can read at grade level. American children of all races and income groups lag behind the children in most industrialized nations in math and science. A Harvard Civil Rights Project/Urban Institute report says only 50 percent of black, 53 percent of Latino, and 75 percent of white students graduated from high school on time with a regular diploma in 2001. A child drops out of high school every ten seconds of every school day. Low-income high school students drop out of school at almost six times the rate of high-income students and black, Latino, and Native American children are more than twice as likely as white children to drop out.

Too many schools fail to inspire, create a passion for learning in children, or embrace children's curiosity when they are young and fresh. Schools that fail to educate and engage students and that implement zero tolerance school discipline policies for nonviolent behaviors are major feeder systems of poor children of color into the prison pipeline. How can it be right, necessary, or sensible for school officials to summon police officers to arrest and handcuff a six-year-old girl in Florida after her temper tantrum or a ten-year-old in Pennsylvania for having scissors in her backpack? Have we adults lost our minds? Younger and younger children are being criminalized for behaviors that used to be handled in the principal's office or with a call to a parent. Mark Reed, a juvenile court administrator in Hamilton County, Ohio, said, "I sat at my desk and I had kids I couldn't even see.... They weren't tall enough. I wondered what in the world could you have done?" Educators must examine and community leaders need to challenge these destructive practices. Children misbehaving in school need help—not expulsion, arrest, and detention.

If we want to assess the status of America's future competitiveness, national security, and democratic health, one need only stop at the school doors through which millions of ill-prepared students pour every day.

What do we do? Educators need to remember what their mission is: educating *children*. Those who use public schools as political patronage and job security rather than as child learning and development sites need to be confronted and ousted. Old interests and ways of doing business need to give way so that children's futures can be protected. While there are many wonderful teachers and schools all over the country, there are very, very few whole school *systems* where *all* children are achieving well. But the Wake County, North Carolina school system is one.

Just because it isn't easy to close the achievement gap between middle-class and poor and minority children doesn't mean that it can't be done. With clear goals and a fierce commitment that *every child attend a quality school,* the Wake County school system, the twenty-second largest in the nation, has raised the achievement of all students and substantially reduced the gap in test scores and graduation rates.

The district, which includes the city of Raleigh, its suburbs, and rural towns, serves 121,000 students. Close to 40 percent are African American or Hispanic. In 1998, the district set a goal of bringing 95 percent of students to grade level on the state's standardized math and reading tests. This is Wake's progress so far:

- From 1995 to 2005, the percentage of African American third to eighth grade students who achieved at grade level doubled—from 40 percent to 80 percent. Hispanic children made similar strides. Overall, in 2005, 91 percent of Wake students scored at grade level.

- The on-time graduation rate for African American students in 2005–2006 was 69.9 percent, significantly higher than the rate nationwide.

◁ That same year, 60.5 percent of Wake's low-income students passed the state's high school end-of-year exams, a much higher proportion than those in other systems in North Carolina.

The Wake County experience demonstrates not just that this *can be done* systemwide but *what it takes.* Here are the keys:

An equitable structure supported by key community leaders: Wake County business, community, and educational leaders have made an ongoing commitment, sometimes against substantial opposition, that all schools be healthy schools and reflect the county's diversity. Initially by race and, more recently, by family income, the system has actively sought to create and maintain the kind of enrollment balance considered critical for successful schools and students. Its policy now is that no school should have more than 40 percent of students receiving free or reduced-price lunches, which means that no school is a single-race, high-poverty school, and poor children attend schools that are majority middle class.

Clear goals: The district established clear achievement goals and created a number of initiatives focused on them, including national certification of its teachers, business partnerships, tutoring programs in local churches, and close monitoring of every school.

Educators, school boards, and communities nationwide routinely *say* they want all children to have a quality education but too often do not make the uncomfortable and unpopular decisions that make this possible and persist over the long haul. Wake County is doing it, and its children and community are benefiting. All communities can and should make a real commitment to fulfill their responsibility to educate every child. Our nation's future depends on it.

It is time for *all* public schools and public school systems to become equitable, child-focused institutions that serve all children with love, respect, competence, high expectations, and committed leadership. Schools must partner with parents and community networks in building the seamless web of support children need. Quality early-childhood programs—Head Start, preschool, child care—should be provided in every community for every child to get ready for school. And the constituencies in each of these areas ought to stop fighting with one another and work together for a seamless high-quality early-childhood system that meets the needs of children and parents. Quality after-school and summer enrichment programs must be available to retain and bolster academic gains during out-of-school time. And parents must do their part to support children's school achievement. Private sector leadership on behalf of public schools is vital, as is a moral framework able to transmit not just skills to our children but a larger sense of purpose, which bubbles up from the vibrancy and quality of teachers and educational leaders.

I recommend that teachers and adults ponder some of the great poet-teacher Gabriela Mistral's wisdom and sense of mission about educating children:

◂ "Everything for the school; very little for ourselves."

◂ "Teach always, in the courtyard and on the street, as if they were the classroom. Teach with your demeanor, expression, and words."

- "Live the beautiful theories. Live with kindness, energy, and professional integrity."

- "Brighten your lessons with beautiful words, with a pertinent story, and relate each piece of knowledge to real life."

- "If we don't achieve equality and culture in the school, where else can such things be required?"

- "A teacher who does not read has to be a bad teacher. She's reduced her job to a mechanical function, by not reviewing herself spiritually."

- "Better an illiterate person should teach, than that a dishonest or unjust person should teach."

- "You should be worthy of your job every day. Occasional successes and exertions are not enough."

- "All the vices and meanness of a community are the vices of its teachers."

- "There is no need to fear correction. A fearful teacher is the worst teacher."

- "Everything can be expressed so long as it's presented properly. Even the harshest reprimand can be made without humiliating or poisoning a soul."

- "It's an intolerable breach of instruction to teach facts without teaching how to learn."

- "In the progress or the discreditation of a school we all have a part."

◄ "The fingers of a potter should be firm and soft and loving, all at the same time."

◄ "All effort that is not sustained is lost."

◄ "It's vital to consider the school not as only *one* person's house, but as everyone's house."

I wish for every child the excitement about teaching and learning reflected by Shakira Brown, the young Harlem Children's Zone teacher going off to Antarctica. I wish for all children in every school district the kind of equitable educational structure and community-wide leadership commitment that is making such a difference in Wake County, North Carolina. Educating all of our children can be done if love and commitment to children guide our actions. I thank all educators who are devoting themselves to preparing and inspiring the next generation and I urge many more young people—especially minority young people and males—to consider the noble calling of teacher as a life choice. It will make such a difference in the lives of countless children left behind and to the future of America.

A DAY IN THE LIFE OF AMERICAN CHILDREN

2	mothers die from complications of pregnancy or childbirth.
4	children are killed by abuse or neglect.
5	children or teens commit suicide.
8	children or teens are killed by firearms.
32	children or teens die from accidents.
78	babies die before their first birthdays.

155	children are arrested for violent crimes.
296	children are arrested for drug crimes.
928	babies are born at low birthweight.
1,154	babies are born to teen mothers.
1,511	public school students are corporally punished.*
2,145	babies are born without health insurance.
2,421	children are confirmed as abused or neglected.
2,467	high school students drop out.*
2,483	babies are born into poverty.
3,477	children are arrested.
4,184	babies are born to unmarried mothers.
18,221	public school students are suspended.

* Based on calculations per school day (180 days of seven hours each).

3

A Letter to Neighbors and Community Leaders

IT TAKES A HERD TO PROTECT
A CHILD: THE BATTLE AT KRUGER PARK

GRANT US YOUR VISION IN OUR TIME

O God, grant us Your vision in our time
Help us to write it so large that even a runner can see it.
Make it so compelling that even a cynic will pause,
so convincing that a skeptic will risk trying to bring hope to others,
and so inspiring that the committed will stand courageously in faith,
leaving the results to You.

One of the most-watched videos on YouTube shows the struggle of a water buffalo family and herd to save a child. It's called the Battle at Kruger Park. It begins with a buffalo mother, father, and child meandering peacefully ahead of the herd, unaware that a pride of six lions are stealthily easing up to attack them. Sensing the danger too late, the water buffalo parents and calf immediately turn and run away. The child cannot keep up. The six swift lions lunge and overpower this slowest and most vulnerable family member, tumbling with him into a river. As the lions attempt to pull the buffalo calf from the water, an alligator grabs one of the child's legs, eager to share the bounty. The tug of war between the lions and alligators over the young buffalo prey seems to last a painful eternity. As the lions win and drag the buffalo child onto land and surround him, ready for the kill, you realize, joyfully, that the child is still alive, but are horrified that he now is going to be devoured.

In the middle of this life-and-death drama, you suddenly hear and then see movement as a large herd of water buffalo—a rescue posse—come storming in to surround the lions, who do not immediately relinquish the child despite being greatly outnumbered. After a moment of herd uncertainty, one angry buffalo—who I just know was the mother—furiously attacks a lion with her horns and hurls him away. Others in the herd follow her lead and confront another lion, but still are unable to extricate the child. Another attempt succeeds as the child struggles to its feet, and the herd swiftly surround and whisk him away. A buffalo remains to chase a remaining lion away. Incredulous that the child was saved, I asked myself: Where is our human posse—our community posse—as the human lions and alligators eat our children alive across America today? And what are the lessons this thrilling rescue of a water buffalo child provide us about our responsibility to protect and save our endangered children?

Protect the most vulnerable first. Powerful predators go after the weakest and the most vulnerable first. Vulnerability is a despised earthly value but a protected and esteemed heavenly one. That is why adults have a special responsibility to shield and guide children until they are able to walk and run and stand on their own and reach successful adulthood. The ultimate test of American democracy, historian Taylor Branch says, "is whether we can protect our voteless, most vulnerable group—children—without whom there is no future." But he also noted our extraordinary debt to those children of America who were frontline soldiers in the civil rights revolution to end racial apartheid. I believe deeply that our unjust neglect of and failure to invest fully in all of our children is the economic and spiritual Achilles' heel that will topple America's leadership in the world in the twenty-first century. I want to yell, "It's the children, stupid!" It's the children— all children—who are the key to a safer, more peaceful and just world order and who are the key to God's kingdom.

Parents alone cannot protect children: it takes a community. There are many lurking dangers that threaten children over which parents have too little control and there is a warning here about what happens when families get out too far from the larger community. Would the six lions have dared attack this bigger buffalo group if they had remained closer together? Would they have seized the child had he been farther back and encircled by adult herd members? The refusal of the parents to abandon their child and their strategic wisdom in seeking help allayed my initial wrong judgment when I saw them flee, leaving the child behind— just as we often judge poor parents who seek help. After the crisis passed, it was clear the two water buffalo parents could not have saved themselves or their child against six lions. They needed others and, unlike so many human parents, they had others willing to help and who saw the child as belonging to their broader community. We humans often tend to distinguish between our own children and other people's children, valuing our own more than others. We do not feel a duty to protect other people's endangered children, especially if it requires inconvenience or sacrifice. These buffalo parents were lucky to be able to return swiftly with a large herd to surround and overpower the six powerful predators accosting their child. The herd's superiority of numbers also was strategic—some were able to grab the child while others attacked and fended off the persistent lions.

Children today are threatened by so many negative forces. Parents alone cannot fight the epidemic gun violence in their communities. Parents alone cannot shut out or withstand our cultural glorification of violence, loveless sex, excessive materialism, and celebrity. Parents alone cannot counter the vile lyrics that make our girls feel they are simply objects to satisfy male desires or the disrespectful labeling of our mothers, sisters, and daughters as "hos and bitches." Parents alone cannot counter messages from peers and entertainment "role models" to many of our sons that prison is a normal, even desired, rite of passage to manhood. While parents must cut off the TV, it takes a community organizing to say *stop* to TV advertisers, producers, and performers to end the disgusting lyrics and trivial messages and lifestyles that corrode our children's values and lead them astray for profit. It will take a herd of caring people to tell the record companies, *Stop!* It will take a herd of young people and parents and faith leaders to say to the gangsta rappers, *Stop!*—we will not buy your music and we will make you pariahs. It will take a herd of leaders and consumers to tell advertisers that we will not buy their products if they continue to support programming with excessive violence or racial and gender stereotyping, which distort our children's views about themselves and other human beings and foster misunderstanding and discord.

In our profit-driven culture, children have become a huge

consumer market relentlessly targeted by corporations who seek to "pimp" them in order to nag and influence their parents to buy their brands and products they do not need and many cannot afford. The herd of neighbors, faith congregations, educators, and community leaders needs to join parents in surrounding the child with positive messages and alternatives to the streets and TV and make children subjects for special care rather than crass exploitation.

You and I must be a herd for children. Our children face so many dangers today from drug peddlers and gangs and pedophiles on the Internet and in institutions charged with protecting and educating them, and from guns and peers who lead them astray. Many poor children who are being sucked into a prison pipeline are bleeding from many wounds and face an accumulation of risks that overwhelm their fragile lives. Family dysfunction results in many children being sent into a broken and underfunded child welfare system, where they face multiple foster care placements and continuing instability. They attend failing schools that don't expect or help them to learn or to build their self-esteem. They live in violent, drug-saturated, and uncaring neighborhoods without health or mental health facilities or quality after-school, summer, and recreational programs. Congregations of faith dot almost as many inner city streets as liquor stores but, unlike liquor stores, their doors are often closed. Where, then, is the beleaguered child to seek protection? The water buffalo story makes clear what the child's fate would have been had there been no rescue. So many bystanders across our nation are letting countless children be devoured by the lions and alligators of drugs and violence and hollow lives. Not my child! Not my fight! Self-interest first! Convenience first! But the parable of the Good Samaritan reminds us that when there is a human life in danger, each of us needs to stop and help, not cross the street, turn a deaf ear and blind eye, and hurry on our way. And it reminds us that everyone is our neighbor.

All great faiths speak to our duty to give preferential protection to the child who is God's messenger of hope and the bearer of the future. Dietrich Bonhoeffer, the great Protestant theologian, believed that the test of the morality of a society is how it treats its children. Our rich nation fails Bonhoeffer's test every hour of every day as we continue to permit a child to be born into poverty every 35 seconds; to be abused or neglected every 36 seconds; to be born without health insurance every 41 seconds; to be killed by a gun every 3 hours; to drop out of school every 10 seconds of every school day; and to be sentenced to the economic and social death of illiteracy by the millions in our globalizing world. Bonhoeffer was a pacifist who believed violence was inconsistent with the Gospel ideals he sought to follow. But he believed the Holocaust posed such a grave threat to humanity and the future that he was required to compromise his purity of conscience and participate in an effort to assassinate Hitler. "How is the coming generation to live?" Bonhoeffer asked. And when he thought of the future, he thought of the child as "quite literally the future of the human race." Every responsible adult needs to ask ourselves Bonhoeffer's question in a world awash with nuclear and conventional weapons whose costs today are a theft from those who are hungry, sick, uneducated, homeless, and hopeless.

We must act with urgency to save children. We need a strategy, the strength of numbers, and an urgent commitment to action when a child faces mortal danger. We lack that sense of urgency in our nation today for the millions of children denied health and mental health care and for children who are deeply endangered by gun violence, sexual abuse, and neglect that destroy or cripple their lives forever. How I wish political leaders did not treat children and their advocates as just another special interest group who must get in line behind powerful and rich defense contractors, drug companies, insurance companies, bankers, provider groups, and special-interest lobbyists to make their case for why children's health, safety, and education needs should be met and given priority in a decent society. Children are dying today, are being born today, and have only one childhood, which is now. In 2009 I hope our nation will not wait until *all* Americans who need and deserve health care get it before covering *all* children. We have been debating universal health care for many decades and I strongly support it. But we must begin with children, who are the most cost-effective group to cover, *now*. They need to have their health and mental health needs diagnosed and treated *now* in order to see the blackboard and hear the teacher and be able to sit still and learn. They need help to overcome their abuse and neglect *now* and should not be left, like thousands of Katrina's children, to struggle with their trauma alone. They are dying from tooth abscesses and preventable illness *now*. As the State Children's Health Insurance Program—SCHIP—comes up for decision in 2009, I urge our president and Congress to follow the American people's wishes and insure *every* child—not one third of them as Congress proposed in 2007—guaranteeing them comprehensive health coverage regardless of the state they live in. I have three sons—how unthinkable it would have been to have to pick only one to receive health coverage when they were growing up.

Never give up on a child. The most important lesson the buffalo story teaches is about the resilience of children and how we must never give up on any child despite the odds. I was amazed to see the buffalo calf struggling to wrest his leg from both the alligator and lions in the water. I am inspired every year by the unbelievable young people the Children's Defense Fund celebrates in a number of cities who survive and thrive and give back to others despite unbelievable obstacles thrown in their way: I have watched as many of them have grabbed the lifeline thrown by one caring grandparent, teacher, counselor, neighbor, or older sibling, and gone on to succeed and become caring parents. They inspire me and others to keep trying to simultaneously change the odds stacked against millions while continuing to rescue as many individual children as possible. Just one person *can* make a difference and save a child's life. Person by person, congregation by congregation, community by community, herd by herd, we can change the treatment of children in our nation and world. I look forward to the day when enough American adults encircle endangered children with as much courage and outrage as the water buffalo in the battle of Kruger Park. Let us affirm, empower, and celebrate children across our land who, despite the unjust odds handed them by the lottery of birth, are living heroic lives. And let us stand together to build the powerful movement required to move all of our children out of harm's way.

A Letter to Faith Leaders

*If any of you put a stumbling block before one of these little ones who
believes in me, it would be better for you if a great millstone were fastened
around your neck and you were drowned in the depth of the sea. Woe to the
world because of stumbling blocks! Occasions for stumbling are bound to
come, but woe to the one by whom stumbling blocks come. . . . It is not the
will of your Father in heaven that one of these little ones should be lost.*

—MATTHEW 18:6–7, 14

*Why was there violence in Gilead? Because they made what is primary
secondary and what is secondary primary. How so? Because they loved
their possessions more than their own children.*

—MIDRASH TANHUMA, MATTOT

A church that does not unite itself to the poor in order to denounce from the place of power, the injustice committed against them is not truly the Church of Jesus Christ.

—EL SALVADORAN ARCHBISHOP OSCAR ROMERO, THE FIRST
BISHOP SLAIN ON THE ALTAR SINCE THOMAS BECKET IN THE
TWELFTH CENTURY

God does instruct you . . . concerning the children who are weak and oppressed; that you stand firm for justice to orphans.

—QUR'AN 4:127

I am a child of the black church—the granddaughter, daughter, sister, and aunt of Baptist ministers. Justice for children and the poor is my ministry because that was what all the Wright children were taught by our parents, church, community, and elders. When my mother died, an old white man in my hometown asked me what I did. I replied that I serve and advocate for children and the poor—exactly what my parents did, just on a different scale and in a different arena.

When I was growing up, the church was the hub of child and community activity. As a black child I couldn't play in public parks or sit down for a soft drink at a drugstore lunch counter, so my daddy and mama built a playground behind our church with a skating rink and snack bar. Black community members gathered at our church to hear Joe Louis's boxing matches on the radio and boys, hoping to become the next heavyweight boxing champion of the world, could experience the racial barrier shattering through will and skill. The church was a lifeline of help and hope for young and old alike, filling in the gaps left by many families struggling to survive in our rural, poor, and segregated community. It did not matter whether you were a church member: if you were a child or an adult with a need, Daddy welcomed all. It sickens me when I hear ministers today refusing to serve needy children because their parents are not members. These are the children who need help most!

Congregations of every faith and race need to open wide their too-often-closed doors during idle summer months, weekends, and after-school hours to provide children positive alternatives to the street, and expose them to positive mentors and caring adults.

My parents, who believed deeply in education and service, would be pleased that our old parsonage in Bennettsville, South Carolina, where I was born, is the curriculum development laboratory for CDF Freedom Schools, summer reading enrichment programs. About a third of the 136 CDF Freedom Schools sites serving about 9,000 children in 2008 are in black churches. During six to eight weeks in the summer, college-age-teacher-mentors teach children their history, culture, and rich legacy of struggle from the Civil Rights Movement. Children learn to serve, to engage in a civic activity, to resolve conflict nonviolently, and to love reading for reading's sake. Parents attend weekly workshops. Freedom Schools train two generations of new leaders: the five-to-fifteen-year-old children in the schools and the college-age teacher-mentors. More than 70,000 children have had a Freedom Schools experience since 1995. Millions need it.

WHAT DO CHILDREN AND YOUTH NEED FROM RELIGIOUS
LEADERS AND PEOPLE OF FAITH TODAY?

They need us to be present and to care—day in and day out—as they struggle to make it through childhood to adulthood, and to lead in reweaving the fabric of community so essential to family stability. They need the integrity of our lived example of what it means to be a person of faith. As the daughter of a father who was an activist minister and of a mother who was chief church fund-raiser, founder of the mother's club, church organist, and choir director, I learned my responsibilities to the poor, elderly, disabled, sick, and young. I went with my parents every Sunday after church to visit and take communion to the sick; to deliver coal and food at Christmas; and to run errands for the elderly and disabled in my community. I would have been devastated if they were not who I thought they were or if they said one thing in church and did another thing in their daily lives. Whenever they saw a need they tried to respond. My mother opened our home to twelve foster children after she raised me and my four siblings and she and my father began a home for the aged, since none existed for black citizens in my hometown, and I had to help care for them.

Children need our caring presence and support when the adults in their families cannot care for, fail, or hurt them. They need our rituals, moral clarity, and examples in a faithful community of disciplined caring. And parents, and increasingly grandparents, need our ongoing support as they try to raise children in these challenging times.

Children need our affirmation when they do well and loving and constructive admonitions when they stray. As a child, how I loved Children's Day every June, when we got new outfits and church applause for memorizing and reciting special poems or Bible passages. Children were community property. I still remember church elders reporting on me and my friends when we were in places we had no business being or were conducting ourselves in ways they knew our parents would not approve. They took care of me when my parents went out of town and sent care packages with fried chicken and biscuits and greasy dollar bills when I went off to college. I strived then and strive now to fulfill their high expectations for me and not to let them down.

Children need assurances that God will never abandon or leave them alone through our unfailing presence as God's surrogates in the world. They need adults to see and speak to, smile at and compliment them. Everywhere I went in my childhood, adults waved and spoke and asked how I was. These simple courtesies and adult recognition meant a lot but are often missing today as many religious people fear young people, keep their doors shut, or close them if they see teens coming.

Children need our continuous countercultural voices, examples, and guidance in a world awash with false prophets spouting false values, and they need constant reminders that they are sacred children of God—each equal to all others. Children of color especially need to know their great heritage and that they are made in the image of God and not BET and the latest American definition of external beauty. Black boys need to know that they are the heirs and sons of Benjamin E. Mays, Martin Luther King Jr., Frederick Douglass, and Benjamin Banneker, and not Snoop Dogg, 50 Cent, or gangsta rappers chasing the almighty dollar. Black girls need to be told they are not objects—just boobs and booties—but the daughters of great heroines like Mrs. Rosa Parks, Sojourner Truth, Harriet Tubman, and Mary McLeod Bethune, and to respect their bodies and deeper inner selves that no one can touch or sully.

Children need faith leaders to speak out against and stop condoning, denying, and glossing over the pervasive domestic violence, child abuse, neglect, and misogyny in our homes, congregations, workplaces, and culture. They need faith communities to be safe havens with safe people and to help parents by teaching in word and deed what it means to be a man, a woman, a loving father and mother, a good provider, and a faithful friend, and how to form and sustain healthy relationships.

Children need Christian faith leaders to work harder to end the reality that eleven a.m. on Sunday morning is still the most segregated time in America. They need to see you and all faiths reaching out to the needy, the stranger, and partnering with congregations and community institutions of different races, ethnicities, and faiths.

Beyond the charity and service all faiths demand, children need faith institutions to speak and stand up to those who treat them unjustly. They need you to challenge rather than mimic the culture, and not pander to leaders who ignore and vote against children's most basic rights to live and learn, to be healthy and safe, and to escape poverty. They need you to hear their desperate cries for help. Black youths in Boston, Massachusetts, were killing one another on the streets until a group of black ministers created the Boston Ten Point Coalition. The catalyst was a church funeral for a slain youth that was interrupted by an opposing gang with guns. A minister friend commented that if the church didn't go out into the streets, the streets would come into the church. So ministers went out into the streets and their efforts decreased and even stopped youth inner-city gun deaths for thirty months.

The faith community has extraordinary power and resources to save children and end poverty if it would mobilize and use them effectively. There are 345,000 houses of worship and religious centers of all faiths in America; 340,000 are Christian churches with more than 155 million members. More than 40,000 are historically black churches with more than 11.5 million members. The rest are Baha'i Spiritual Assemblies, synagogues, Islamic masjids, Sikh gurdwaras, and Hindu and Buddhist temples. There are 13 million poor children in America; 9.4 million children who lack health insurance; and 900,000 children who are victims of abuse and neglect every year. About 100,000 children are detained annually in juvenile detention institutions and 1.5 million have an incarcerated parent. Imagine the positive impact on child suffering in America. . . .

◄ If each one of these faith groups and communities committed to reaching out to ten at-risk poor families, working with juvenile court and child welfare officials to identify and prevent removal of children from their families or their placement in detention.

◄ If half raised their voices to stop our morally obscene federal budget policies that cut investments in and services to poor children to give tax cuts to millionaires and agreed to work on achieving *one* major child policy change each year: health care in 2009; child poverty reduction in 2010.

◄ If a third of them encouraged one member to adopt one child from foster care with promised support from other members. All the 125,000 children in foster care waiting to be adopted could have a loving permanent family.

◄ If two tenths of 1 percent of all Christians in the United States became foster parents, with other congregation members offering respite care and other support. The more than 300,000 children who enter foster care each year could achieve greater stability until they could be reunified with their own families or an adoptive family could be found, rather than being shunted from one foster home to another with the increased likelihood of ending up in the juvenile and criminal justice systems.

◄ If a third of these congregations agreed to create a network of mentors and families to offer ongoing support to youths aging out of foster care or returning to the community after being discharged from a juvenile detention facility or prison who need surrogate families. The more than 20,000 youths who age out of foster care each year without being returned to a family or being adopted and the 97,000 youths in secure juvenile detention facilities would have a welcoming lifeline back to their community until they could stand on their own feet.

◄ If even 10 percent sponsored a quality summer or after-school program to provide children a positive alternative to the streets or if a cluster of congregations got together and sponsored six- to eight-week quality summer programs for children rather than just a week of vacation Bible or religious school. They could engage many thousands of children in positive activities and show them a faith that serves rather than just preaches.

◄ If another 10 percent provided after-school homework centers with tutoring and snacks funded by the federal government topped off with fun and games for some of the millions of children who come home to no one and face great temptations. We could save and help mold countless young lives by placing books and computers in their hands and encouraging words in their ears.

⊰ If each faith leader encouraged members to volunteer as a mentor once a month for a child under the jurisdiction of the child welfare and juvenile justice systems, it would change many children's lives.

⊰ If one tenth of our congregations partnered with local schools or other community institutions to sponsor a "Beat the Odds" Award ceremony each year to celebrate and encourage young people who are succeeding in their communities despite enormous hardships by giving them scholarships and encouragement to go to and stay in college. Numerous children could be rerouted to successful adulthood and away from incarceration and we could change the attitudes of adults and other youth about the positive potential of young people so many write off.

A theologian friend, Dr. Eileen Lindner, shared the story of taking her car to a Jiffy Lube for servicing. Not having anything to read, she picked up a manual on the coffee table about boating. A chapter on the rules for what happens when boats encounter one another on the open sea described two kinds of craft: burdened and privileged. The craft with power that can accelerate and push its way through the waves, change direction, and stop on demand is the burdened one. The craft dependent on the forces of nature, wind, tide, and human effort to keep going is the privileged craft. Since powerful boats can make their way forward under their own power, they are burdened with responsibility to give the right of way to the powerless or privileged vessels dependent on the vagaries of the tide, wind, and weather. "Who wrote this thing?" Eileen asked. "Billy Graham? Mother Teresa? What's going on in our land when the New Jersey State Department of Transportation knows that the powerful must give way if the powerless are to make safe harbor and the government of the United States and the Church of Jesus Christ and other people of God are having trouble with the concept?"

For many years the Children's Defense Fund has worked with congregations of all faiths to encourage them to strengthen their services to at-risk children and to rekindle their public voice for justice for children and the poor. For eighteen years, with the sponsorship of a broad multifaith advisory board, we have sponsored Children's Sabbaths each October, a national weekend of observance, prayer, worship, and renewed commitment to children in which thousands of congregations of all faiths participate. Multifaith manuals are prepared annually to aid worship, education, action, and other activities in churches, synagogues, masjids, gurdwaras, Baha'i communities, Hindu and Buddhist temples, and other places of worship.

Every third week of July at the former Alex Haley Farm, CDF's center for spiritual, character, and leadership development near Knoxville, Tennessee, we convene the annual Samuel DeWitt Proctor Institute for Child Advocacy Ministry, now in its fourteenth year. A song we sing at the institute includes the divine promise, "I will do a new thing in you . . ." Each day, each moment we have the opportunity to do the new thing to which God calls us as we transform our places of worship, communities, nation, world—and especially ourselves—to extend the love, respect, compassion, and justice that all our children need and deserve everywhere.

For the ways that so many people of faith are working already to manifest that vision of our world made new for the sake of our children, I am grateful. And for the urgent hard work we have yet to do to make our nation a safe harbor for every child and to end poverty, I extend a call for your stronger partnership and unwavering voice in building a movement to ensure that not even one of our little ones is lost and that *all* children are able to live the life our Creator intends.

A PLEA FOR GOD TO SAVE CHILDREN

O God, please save our children because they are so small.

O God, please save our children because they are so weak and defenseless.

O God, please save our children because so many are neglected and abused.

O God, please save our children because so many are ravaged by hunger and sickness.

O God, please save our children because so many are killed by violence and war and poverty and dirty water.

O God, please save our children who are abandoned by adults and cannot save themselves.

O God, please speak for our children whose cries are unheard and whose silent tears are ignored.

O God, please stand for our children in a world of adults who stand against them.

O God, please open the hardened hearts and eyes of all who resist knowing and doing what knowing compels to heal the hurting young in our world.

A Letter to Young People: Anchors and Sails for Life's Voyage

THE MEASURE OF SUCCESS

God, help our children to learn what is real. Help them not to defer to people because they are powerful or rich but because they are good or wise or helpful or loving.

Help them not to defer to people because they are attractive or famous but because they share a mission, a life view, a commitment to something bigger than themselves.

Help them not to defer to people because of race or gender but because they are principled and honest.

It is the responsibility of adults to share with you in the next generation what we think is important. You can take or leave our advice as you see fit. Here is a bit of mine that I hope you find useful as you set out to navigate the exciting sea of life.

⌒

You are far more than any test can measure. No test can predict the quality and worth of your life or the contributions you can make. In this era of No Child Left Behind, standardized tests, and college admissions stress, I want you to remember that no test can measure many of the most important strengths you may have and need to succeed. While it is important to try to do as well as possible on tests, they do not measure your motivation and work ethic; your character; your courage and perseverance; your honesty, manners, and follow-through; or your caring, kindness, and willingness to serve others. Dr. Martin Luther King Jr. did not perform at all well on his Graduate Record Examination (except in literature). Yet in the same months he received his test results, one of his theology professors at Crozer Theological Seminary wrote a letter supporting his application for further graduate school education, saying he was "one of the most brilliant students Crozer ever had." He was his class graduation speaker, and president of the student body; he had a golden tongue and a grasp of philosophy and of the Bible sufficient to transform a nation. He was our greatest twentieth-century American prophet and perhaps our greatest twentieth-century world prophet.

And we all should know by now that "intelligence" has nothing to do with wisdom, common sense, compassion, and effectiveness. Brilliant people created the nuclear weapons that have brought us to the edge of extinction. Traditionally smart people have taken us to war, fabricating stories of weapons of mass destruction. Purportedly intelligent people run the corporations and formulate the government policies that help create the misery and suffering of billions at home and around the world and seem to think it is all right for the rich to take from the poor, to bomb children in order to save them, and to kill people in order to make them free.

Find your gifts—however few or many they may be—and build on them. You have them. God gave them to you. Do not let any man or woman take them away or squeeze them into a tiny box labeled IQ. Make sure you develop not only your intelligence quotient but also your spiritual, physical, emotional, and leadership quotients that make up your whole person.

You do not always have to win to win. Sometimes losing is winning and sometimes winning is losing. Abraham Lincoln believed "the probability that we may fail in the struggle ought not deter us from the support of a cause we believe to be just." And how you win can be as important as what you win. If you have to lie or cheat to win, you lose. If you have to humiliate or demean your opponent to win, you lose. If you have to violate core principles to win, then you might want to weigh carefully whether winning is worth it. And if in your pursuit of immediate individual victory, you hurt or destroy bigger or more important collective interests over the long term, you need to pause and make hard choices about who you are and who you want to be.

Do your part, however small. "I would guess there is at least an 85 percent certainty that humanity will wipe itself out in the reasonably near future—but I put my faith in the remaining 15 percent," Leo Szilard, an early atomic scientist, said. Be part of the 15 percent. A friend commented that "the world is held together by the compassion and commitment and talent and love of a very few people." What more could you or I ask than to be one of them? I love the Chinese tale about an elephant who saw a hummingbird lying on its back with its tiny feet up in the air.

"What are you doing?" the elephant asked. The hummingbird replied, "I heard the sky might fall today, and so I am ready to help hold it up, should it fall." The elephant laughed and said cruelly, "Do you really think those tiny feet could help hold up the sky?" The hummingbird kept his feet up in the air intent on his purpose as he replied, "Not alone. But each must do what he can. And this is what I can do." Do what you can.

Give a good day. I often am so preoccupied with having a good or a productive day that I forget to help make another's day good with a kind word, a thoughtful deed, thanks for a job well done, or a call or visit. I have a number of dear friends in their eighties and nineties whom I love and admire very much. A call can cheer them—and me—up. Everybody needs to be remembered, especially those who are living alone or who are shut in for long periods of the day.

Be a sower. Keep planting and watering seeds of hope and help. Don't let others discourage you. I love Ruth Krauss's children's book *The Carrot Seed*, about a little boy who planted a carrot seed. His mother said, "I am afraid it won't come up." His father said, "I'm afraid it won't come up." And his big brother said, "It won't come up." Every day the little boy pulled up the weeds around the seed and sprinkled the ground with water. But nothing came up. And nothing came up. Everyone kept saying it wouldn't come up. But he still pulled up the weeds around it every day and sprinkled the ground with water. And then, one day, a carrot came up just as the little boy had known it would. For thirty-five years the Children's Defense Fund has been planting and watering as many seeds as possible for children and pulling up the endless weeds that crop up over and over again, trying to choke them. Some have blossomed into health care and child care and education, a chance to escape poverty, and adoptive homes for millions of children; some have died in the harsh heat of politics and the ice of indifference. But we must and will keep planting and planting enough seeds until every child is welcomed at our nation's table of plenty and has the basic necessities of life required to survive and thrive. Seeds do not sprout overnight. They take time and tending. Gardener Henry David Thoreau said: "Though I do not believe that a plant will spring up where no seed has been, I have great faith in a seed. . . . Convince me that you have a seed there, and I am prepared to expect wonders."

Just do the work and don't worry about the credit. Former Indian prime minister Indira Gandhi said her grandfather once told her that there were two kinds of people: those who do the work and those who take the credit. He told her to try to be in the first group; there was much less competition. Often those at the press conference or hogging the spotlight are not the ones who do most of the work. Most change is hard, unexciting, behind-the-scenes grunt work that takes follow-through, attention to detail, and pushing, pushing, and pushing until the hard walls of resistance to change crumble.

Be humble and grateful for life. It is a loan from God and not an entitlement. Pay your rent of thanks through joy and true service to others. You have been created by and made in the image of God. Everything we have comes from God. Rejoice and be glad in it but don't forget to whom you—and every human being—belong. Don't put on airs or confuse external honors and trappings with internal virtue. We are all sinners and imperfect human beings. And don't forget to say thanks to those who helped you along life's way. Bernard of Clairvaux, a twelfth-century French mystic, said:

"You can frequently see in the church men sprung from lower ranks who have attained to the higher, and who from being poor have become rich, beginning to swell with pride, forgetting their low extraction, becoming ashamed of their family and disdaining their parents because they are in a humble condition. You can also see wealthy men attaining rapidly to ecclesiastical honors, and then at once regarding themselves as men of great holiness though they have changed their clothes only and not their minds." Don't be like them. Thank your parents and grandparents and others who kept you out of harm's way and sacrificed to give you a better life.

Struggle, struggle, struggle to develop a nonviolent heart in our violent culture and world. "Nonviolence," Mahatma Gandhi said, "is not a garment to be put on and off at will. Its seat is in the heart and it must be an inseparable part of our being." This is very, very hard in our nation and world, where violence is pandemic in our interpersonal relationships, within and among our nation-states, and is glorified in our media. There are so few courses in our congregations or schools at any level on nonviolent conflict resolution but if they are offered in your school, take them. If they are not offered, ask your principal or academic dean to develop them. Gandhi believed that if we are to have peace in the world we must begin with the young. Maria Montessori thought that the very purpose of education was to teach peace. "Establishing lasting peace is the work of education; all politics can do is keep us out of war," she said.

Learn to be still and listen to the silence within you. It takes much personal discipline to learn to be still and try to find your authentic self. I constantly struggle to find sufficient quiet time for my mind to turn off outward things so I can try to listen in silence for the genuine within. In this era of constant electronic communication, it is even more difficult, but I believe it is worthwhile. Carlo Caretto, the desert father and author of *I, Francis*, reminded all of us of the need to preserve a place of stillness to listen to and be renewed by God. This is very hard as many of us become addicted to our false sense of indispensability.

Live as if you like yourself. It might happen. Live as if you like others. It might happen. Nobody's perfect. So don't get hung up seeking perfection in yourself and in others. Attitude so often determines outcome. Avoid sour and dour people. Life's much too short. We need every bit of encouragement we can get and we need to give it.

Be prepared to sacrifice and persevere for what you believe. Our culture touts cheap bargains, quick fixes, easy answers, and feel-good instant gratification. *Sacrifice* is almost an extinct word. Each of us must determine to be less greedy and wasteful and hold our leaders accountable for being so. And please vote. Voting and participating in community civic life helps keep democracy, which is not a spectator sport, alive. Run for elective office if you want a better life for children—especially for school boards—and please remember children *after* you get elected.

Do not die before you die. See and listen. Bask in the countless miracles and beauty all around you. Stay awake and alert to the incredible currents of life everywhere every minute—the laughter of children, the breathtaking panoramas of color in the sky and in flora and fauna, the cooing sounds of doves, the magic of music, the gentle ripples in a pond and the dancing reflections of trees surrounding it, the lush shades of green mosses decorating trees along remote paths, morning birds' song, the veins of a beautiful leaf, the smiling pansy faces, the graceful landing of geese in water, the stately ancient trees genuflecting to the sun, and fields of sunflowers whose petals are uncountable. Thoreau lived for more than two years in the woods at Walden Pond "because I wished to live deliberately, to front only the essential facts of life and see if I could learn what it had to teach, and not, when I come to die, discover that I had not lived."

Try to follow rather than simply admire God's messengers. Danish philosopher Søren Kierkegaard wrote that Christ never asked for admirers but for disciples: "His whole life on earth, from beginning to end, was destined solely to have followers and to make admirers impossible.... He came to be the *pattern*.... A follower is or strives to be what he admires. An admirer, however, keeps himself personally detached." Many more Americans would rather admire and celebrate than follow Dr. King or Mahatma Gandhi's calls for nonviolence and sacrifice. I hope you learn as much about these great men as you can and follow them.

Don't be selfish and forget those left behind. When Harriet Tubman escaped from slavery in Maryland to freedom in Pennsylvania, she "felt like [she] was in heaven." But she immediately felt a wider sense of mission: "I had crossed the line, I was free; but there was no one to welcome me to the land of freedom. I was a stranger in a strange land; and my home, after all, was down in Maryland.... But I was free and they should be free. I would make a home in the North and bring them there, God helping me." She went back south nineteen times, rescuing at least three hundred slaves, and boasted that she never lost a passenger on her very dangerous Underground Railroad. Those of us who have been fortunate enough to rise to the top need to reach back and bring others with us. If the bottom keeps getting bigger it will bring the top down.

Do the best you can with what you have. United States Supreme Court Justice Thurgood Marshall's chosen epitaph for his life was "I did the best I could with what I had." Don't dwell on what you lack; dwell on what you have and use it to the fullest with gratitude. Don't dwell on your failures—learn from them and move on. Don't dwell on your fears or sorrows—dwell on your hopes. Don't make excuses. Don't hide behind racism or sexism or anything else if you haven't done your best.

It's okay to say "I don't know." Take time to think, inquire, and reflect and then make the best decision you can based on what you can discern. Do not let your peers, the media or political leaders, or anyone else hurry or force-feed you into wrong solutions to wrong problems for the wrong reasons. Once you get in the habit of pretending you know what you don't, you're headed for anxiety and trouble. It's okay to ask as many questions as you need to to make sound judgments.

Life is not just or mostly about happiness. Dr. W.E.B. DuBois, one of our greatest scholars, echoed my own father's beliefs in an address he gave to Howard University graduates in 1939. He said: "To increase abiding satisfaction for the mass of our people and for all people, someone must sacrifice something of his own happiness. This is a duty only to those who recognize it as a duty. It is silly to tell intelligent human beings: Be good and you will be happy. The truth is today, be good, be decent, be honorable and self-sacrificing, and you will not always be happy. You will often be desperately unhappy. You may even be crucified, dead, and buried. And the third day you will be just as dead as the first. But, with the death of your happiness may easily come increased happiness and satisfaction and fulfillment for other people—strangers, unborn babes, uncreated worlds. If this is not sufficient incentive, never try it—remain hogs."

Be kind. A welcoming smile, gesture, or word can mean so much to another, especially a child younger than you are who will look up to you, an older person hungering for attention, or a new person who needs to be put at ease. During President Nelson Mandela's state visit to our country, to my absolute astonishment I found myself seated at his right hand during a luncheon in his honor at the United States Department of State. After he greeted all those at the table—many his old friends—he sat down and greeted me with a warm smile. He then took my hand in his and held it for several minutes on his knee in a grandfatherly gesture of warmth and friendship I will forever cherish. Remember how you felt when you moved to a new school or neighborhood and were looking for new friends or were in an unforeseen or uncomfortable situation and someone smiled at or spoke kindly to you or made a thoughtful gesture?

Don't be afraid to leave comfortable shores. Life's a very big and beautiful sea even if it does get scary sometimes. Explore as much of it as you can. But make sure your boat is seaworthy: your anchor is onboard, your sails are in good shape, your life vest is on, and somebody knows where you are! One of the very best times of my life was studying and traveling abroad during my junior year of college when I spent twelve months in France and Switzerland, and traveled to other countries for three months. I learned at nineteen that I could navigate the world alone. I spent a summer in the Soviet Union with a Lisle Fellowship student group soon after the Iron Curtain was lifted and it began letting foreigners in. I got to meet Premier Khrushchev and got drunk for the first time in my life in his presence (it was *no* fun the next day!). And I was glad, when I visited South Africa while rigid racial apartheid was still in force, that I snuck into a hospital to visit the late great freedom fighter Robert Sobukwe, banned by South African authorities, to take him a message from his daughter, who was living in the United States. His peaceful radiance, although he was dying, reflected a man whose life's work was well done.

Keep saying the truth and holding on to your beliefs even if it appears no one is listening. A rabbi, who lived and preached a life of virtue while his congregation ignored him and went on with their selfish ways, was asked: "Rabbi, why do you bother? Nobody listens. You're not changing anything." And the rabbi replied: "But you misunderstand. I don't do it to change them. I do it to keep them from changing me." Try not to let the world tell you who you are. Try to tell the world who you are and don't be a copycat. God made you an original.

Don't give up too soon or before you have done your best and even better than your best. "Nothing," Nobel Peace Prize Laureate and Chicago settlement house pioneer Jane Addams said, "could be worse than the fear that one had given up too soon and left one unexpended effort which might have saved the world." There have been many times when I have wanted to give up. In the midst of a steep uphill battle to get Congress to pass and President George H. W. Bush to sign a child-care bill, I wanted to throw in the towel when several important liberal friends in Congress unexpectedly pursued an alternative bill making it very hard to hold together a broad child-care coalition. In despair I left Washington for an Outward Bound expedition in Maine. When I saw the ropes course, I was overwhelmed and thought I could not do it. But focusing on getting from point A to point B until I traversed each challenge and reached the end rekindled my confidence to return to Washington and keep fighting. With allies, CDF focused point by point on each political obstacle facing the child-care bill until it passed and President Bush signed it against great odds in 1990—nineteen years after a more comprehensive child development act we had developed had been passed by Congress but was vetoed by President Nixon.

Aim high and work very hard to reach your goal. Thoreau said: "If you have built castles in the air, your work need not be lost; that is where they should be. Now put the foundations under them." I admire so many of the high school students the Children's Defense Fund celebrates each year who beat the odds and overcome incredible obstacles of family violence, parental incarceration, drug abuse, homelessness, and illness and go on to college, succeed, and give back. Many are now teachers, doctors, Peace Corps volunteers, lawyers, and journalists. They are daily reminders that no one has a right to give up on any young person. And please do not give up on yourself—*ever*.

Serve. Do something for others and pass on an Earth better than you found it, like missionary doctor, musician, and Nobel Peace Prize Laureate Albert Schweitzer. He believed: "It's not enough merely to exist. It's not enough to say, 'I'm earning enough to live

and support my family. I do my work well. . . . I'm a good church-
goer.' That's all very well, but one must do something more.
Seek always to do some good somewhere. Every man has to seek
in his own way to make his own self more noble." My parents
instilled in me their belief that service is the rent each of us pays
for living—the very purpose of life and not something you do
in your spare time or after you've made your first million or
achieved a desired professional goal or have more time. I'm so
grateful for their guidance and example.

Choose work that promotes life not death. My father told me as a
child that God runs a full employment economy and that if you
just look for and follow the need you'll never lack a purposeful
existence. His advice worked in my life. Many of our brightest
college, graduate school, and professional school graduates each
year take jobs designing weapons or working for corporations
that produce and sell tobacco, guns, and other products that kill
or are of little positive use to people. How much of our war
machinery today is propelled by the need to keep employed the
scientists and the engineers who specialize in weapons of mass
destruction? How much safer might the world become if you
and your peers chose to become scientists or mathematicians
or engineers or economists committed to finding ways to feed
the world's hungry or to finding cures for diseases afflicting the
poor or to assuring there's enough water in dry places or to
teaching children science and mathematics and engineering
skills for nonmilitary jobs in our globalizing world—areas in
which American children lag behind their peers in other industrialized countries. Ask whether the education or job you seek or
get will benefit others and not just yourself and make the world

better or less so. And don't just work for money or power. They won't save your soul or help you sleep at night.

Do not fear criticism or let others define you. "If I answered all criticism, I'd have time for nothing else," Dr. Martin Luther King Jr. said. He echoed Abraham Lincoln, who sought to make his enemies his friends, even bringing some of them into his cabinet, and who tried to hold our warring nation's citizens together in a spirit of charity for all and enmity for none. Nor did Dr. King let labels intended by ill-wishers seeking to discredit him as a radical or extremist succeed. He defined himself and turned them into positives. "When you are right you cannot be too radical; when you are wrong, you cannot be too conservative," he said. Asked about segregationists who called him an extremist, he responded, "I would like to think of myself as an extremist for love." He was not deterred from speaking out against the Vietnam War in his memorable Riverside speech despite the opposition of almost all his friends. And he refused to cancel the Poor People's Campaign when many of his senior staff and board raised strong opposition. Although *liberal* is a dirty word to some, I wear it proudly. But I also wear the label of conservative proudly as I struggle to live the dictates of my faith and conserve the enduring values of right and wrong, family, community, and hard work instilled by my parents and mentors. And I am radical about stopping the preventable suffering of children.

Recognize that you are a global citizen and must compete with peers from China, Japan, India, and all around the globe. Inform yourself about our world and its people. We are all interdependent. Lone ranger capitalism and American hubris wrapped in democratic rhetoric will not succeed. Dr. King said, "Whether we realize it or not, each of us lives eternally in the red. We are everlasting debtors to known and unknown men and women. When we arise in the morning, we go into the bathroom where we reach for a sponge which is provided for us by a Pacific Islander. We reach for soap that is created for us by a European. Then at the table we drink coffee which is provided for us by a South American, or tea by a Chinese or cocoa by a West African. Before we leave for our jobs we are already beholden to more than half of the world.... All life is interrelated. Whatever affects one directly affects all indirectly."

Dream beyond the moment. When I was a young black girl growing up in the segregated South, I always bristled when others sought to limit where I could go and what I could do and be because I was black and female. I always dreamed outside the box and knew I would challenge racial and gender discrimination with every fiber of my being throughout my whole life.

Faith and doubt are twins. Watch out for people who claim they have the only right way and truth. In this world of quick sound bites, think critically about what you hear and read. Dr. King struggled all his life in faith despite deep and continuing doubts and discouragement, constantly urging his followers to stay the course regardless of the political or economic weather. "We must have faith that things will work out somehow, that God will make a way for us when there seems no way," he told the Montgomery black community, at wit's end after 381 days of its boycott and just before a federal court outlawed segregation in public transportation. The first time I heard him speak in Sisters Chapel at Spelman College, he told us students to take the first step for justice in faith even if we could not see the whole staircase and to leave the rest to God. In that same speech he told us to keep moving forward and never give in to despair: "If you cannot fly, drive; if you cannot drive, run; if you cannot run, walk; if you cannot walk, crawl. But keep moving. Keep moving."

Do not give in to that which is easy or convenient. Live intentionally and mindful of the impact of your actions on others. My wonderful colleague Barbara Best told me: The administrator of the Catholic Worker House in Houston once told her that the great sin of our society is the sin of convenience. In our haste to get what we want quickly and easily, we do not acknowledge the impact that we are having on others. The clothes we buy, the shoes we wear, the food we eat, and the cars we drive are all choices that impact the well-being of others. We are called to live mindfully, always thinking about the impact of our actions on others and always seeking to promote harmony and not pain in others in our local communities and around the globe.

A Letter to My Grandchildren, Ellika, Zoe, Elijah, and Levi

What joy you have brought into my and Papa's life. I continuously asked God to bless me to see my children grow up and I am grateful beyond words that God also has blessed me to see you—my children's children. How lucky Papa and I are to have the children we have and how lucky you are to have the parents you have. I am *so* proud of them all and of you. And I want to thank you, Ellika, my firstborn grandchild, for the snazzy name you gave me—La La—which I love *a lot!*

Your parents are doing a really fine job teaching you right and wrong, how to respect yourself and others, to be honest and kind, to be helpful, and to be mindful of your environment. They are encouraging you to be the very special yous that only you can be. If you follow your parents' guidance and examples, you will grow up to be good and purposeful human beings. But I want to share a few wishes for you. Please know you are loved unconditionally and forever like my Joshua, Jonah, and Ezra. There is *nothing* you or any grandchild can ever do that could take my love away. God loves you too with an everlasting and unchanging love and will always catch you if you surrender your life and seek to live faithfully and justly.

So here are some of La La's wishes for you, my very beloved grandchildren.

I wish you:

An optimistic and determined spirit. Helen Keller, who became deaf and blind shortly after her birth, said, "No pessimist ever discovered the secret of the stars or sailed to an uncharted land, or opened a new doorway for the human spirit." She learned to read and function and inspire the world without letting disability dim her spirit. Stay away from pessimistic and cynical people and seek out friends who are positive and encouraging.

A courageous and just spirit willing to speak up for right and against wrong. Being courageous is not being unafraid. It is being able to do what you have to do even when you are afraid. Stand up for what is just even if you are the only one. It is always the right time to do right. One of the proudest moments in my life was waiting with you, Ellika, when you were four years old on the steps of our nation's Capitol for Mrs. Rosa Parks to arrive. In the beautiful twilight of a perfect day, a bus draped in black symbolizing the Montgomery Bus Boycott arrived followed by the hearse carrying Mrs. Parks moving very slowly past very long lines of people circling the Capitol waiting to say thanks and farewell to her. As the integrated military honor guard lifted Mrs. Parks up the Capitol steps in precise cadences toward the rotunda where the President of the United States, leaders of Congress, and other dignitaries awaited her—an unassuming black seamstress who had the courage to sit down for justice and make all America stand up—I squeezed you tight and whispered through tears of gratitude: *"Never ever forget what one committed black woman—one single person—can do."*

A forgiving spirit. "Hate is a very heavy burden to carry," my namesake and great singer Marian Anderson said. Booker T. Washington, the great president of Tuskegee Institute, urged us never to let anybody drag us so low as to make us hate them. Don't let resentments build up and calcify. Free yourself by forgiving yourself and others.

A fair spirit. Don't ask others to do what you are not willing to do yourself and do not treat others as you would not like for them to treat you. This is the basic rule of every great faith.

A zestful spirit and robust conscience. Never lose your sense of wonder and appreciation for life, and don't give or lend your conscience to anybody. Resist the tendency to go along and get along in a world where so much injustice thrives. Don't be a cultural or crowd puppet.

A respectful spirit. You are a sacred child of God. So is every other child and human being. Neither you nor they have any right to look down on anyone because of race, religion, family, gender, place of birth, or any physical characteristic. Do not tell or let others tell unkind jokes in your presence that are intended to hurt or disrespect others.

An imaginative spirit. Don't let external circumstances dictate or dampen your internal dreams and vision. Dr. Mary McLeod Bethune envisaged Bethune Cookman College, a school she would build for black students, when she had only a dump site and $5.00 to begin. When you are forced to endure unpleasant circumstances or setbacks, keep your mind focused on where you aspire to be and will be one day.

A passionate and persevering spirit. Find and pursue your passion. Your great-grandfather Arthur Wright told me I could do and be anything I wanted to be if I dreamed and worked hard enough for it. Don't let closed doors deter you. Keep knocking on them. Cathy Hughes, the black owner of Radio One and TV One, was born in a Nebraska housing project and became a teen mother. Determined to build a better life for herself and her son, she worked hard to realize her passionate love for radio. She seized every opportunity to learn the radio business and did a very good job working her way up. When she tried to borrow money to buy her own station, she faced thirty-two turndowns by white male bankers. But she tried a thirty-third time and succeeded with a Puerto Rican woman banker at Chemical Bank.

A can-do spirit devoted to making a positive difference in the lives of others. And you don't have to wait until you are a grown-up to make a difference. Anne Frank, who lost her life in Hitler's evil Holocaust, said: "How wonderful it is that nobody need wait a single moment before starting to improve the world." We'll read *The Diary of Anne Frank* when you get older as well as many more of the books about child heroines who were courageous nonviolent soldiers in the Civil Rights Movement that changed America. Six-year-old Ruby Bridges walked through screaming and hateful white mobs to the public school she desegregated in New Orleans, stopping daily to pray for them. La

La is proud to have been one of several hundred college students who sat-in and went to jail to protest segregated public accommodations in the South. You take for granted that you can eat and sit and play anywhere you choose but La La could not when I was growing up. It was wonderful to be a part of making America more free and just.

A spirit of pride in your heritage that is very rich and diverse, like the world in which you are growing up. I don't mean pride that seeks to set you above others but pride in and acceptance of who you are. You are all of mixed race (like I'll bet countless other Americans are!). Papa and La La also come from different faith traditions. But what a wonderful chance to learn about and practice my Christian faith and Papa's Jewish traditions and the courageous history of two peoples who survived enslavement, persecution, and discrimination. Being proud of your heritage means respecting other people's heritage, of which they should be equally proud. *Never* deny or be ashamed of who you are!

An unbridled spirit. Think for yourself. I *love* your endless questions and inquiring minds and hope you'll retain a rich curiosity all your lives. It's harder today to resist being carbon copies in America's cookie-cutter consumer culture that spouts so many messages not worth hearing and products seeking to rein in rather than unleash your imagination. Pots and pans and old tin cans and made-up games that cost little or nothing and walks and daydreaming were great fun when I was growing up. Keep up your important tasks of childhood play and let your imaginations soar.

A reverent spirit full of wonder—with eyes, ears, and heart open to the miracles of beauty all around you. The most beautiful things in life are free: sunrises and sunsets, rainbows—especially double ones!—fields of wildflowers, ripples in a pond, the ocean's roar, the choruses of bird songs and children singing, a child's cooing and smile, the breeze, and the dances of trees. Love and protect nature. Listen to and really see it. I'm always amazed at how much I do not see in my busyness and preoccupation. So be still and just be as often as you can.

A grateful spirit. Be grateful to your parents, who gave life to you, and to God, who created all things, people, and the Earth. Pray. Prayer comes in forms too numerous to name: words, song, dance, silence, walking for justice, kind hands helping others. Pray for those with greater needs and for those who have been lanterns in your life. And when you pray for yourselves and your own family, also pray for all the children in our nation and world who need food, safety, a place to stay, education, and somebody to care about them, which you are blessed to have.

A humble yet confident spirit. Since all comes from our Creator, how can one not be humble and share your gifts with others? La La was told over and over by your great-grandparents: "To whom much is given, much is expected." Give back.

A diligent and helpful spirit. Work hard. Earn your keep. Do your share without being asked. Keep asking, "Can I help you?"

A forthright spirit. Ask for what you need and don't let resentment or anger build up because you think your needs were not seen or met. It took me a very long time to figure out that Papa was not able to read my mind although I thought he should be able to. Tell your parents and friends and others what you need and say—nicely—what you like and don't like. La La thinks there would be a whole lot more happy marriages and friendships and professional relations if we didn't expect others to be mind readers and guess what we want or see when we need help.

A generous spirit. Don't spend all the money you earn or receive on yourself. La La gave each of you three coin banks as Christmas-Hanukkah gifts. One is inscribed for spending, one for saving, and one for sharing.

An honest spirit. All of us lie, or twist or spin the truth sometimes, but we should try hard not to and apologize when we do. Try to be truthful even if nobody around you is. Be an example for others. Don't engage in dishonest conduct just to be popular, get along, or get ahead. You don't want friends who try to make you do things that are unsafe or hurtful to others or who lower the standards your parents have taught you.

A joyful spirit. La La's sense of humor needs a lot of work! I need to laugh a lot more and take myself and my work much less seriously. That's why I love being with you all so much—you make me laugh and have fun and forget my idolatrous addiction to carrying the world on my shoulders! I am a groupie of South African archbishop Desmond Tutu, who I think has the most joyous bubbly giggle in the whole world and such a radiant smile.

A compassionate spirit. Listen. See. Hear. Feel. Seek to understand. Care. Share with those in need. If you try to live a life of compassion and faith that seeks justice, God will smile on you.

A curious spirit. Read! Read! Read and explore as much as you can so that you can bask in the full panoramic canvas of our incredible world. Books are a window to all the world and its people. Go to as many places in the world to meet all the real people behind those in the books when you get bigger. Try to be at home everywhere for you will find human beings share many of the same dreams. I am so proud that your parents and Uncle Ez are big readers and travelers.

A nonviolent spirit. I hope you and every child will learn that violence is wrong and will never use it against another. If you are ever abused by anyone—physically or emotionally—please realize it is not your fault but that of the perpetrator. Don't let anyone scare you into silence—seek help, for it is too big a burden for any person to carry alone. I grew up in an era of spanking at home and at school and had to wean myself from this tradition with my own children. When you get bigger, you will learn a lot more about heroes like Dr. Martin Luther King Jr., Mahatma Gandhi, Leo Tolstoy, and Mrs. Fannie Lou Hamer, who taught us how to be nonviolent like Jesus Christ.

A resilient spirit. Don't dwell on your failures. Learn from them and move on. It does not matter how many times you fall down, keep getting up. You are going to make mistakes but try not to keep making the same ones. Don't dwell on your weaknesses or on what you wish you could do but can't. Do what you can do. Build on your strengths. You have many that are unique to you. Don't compare yourself to your sister or brother or cousins or friends or parents or grandparents. Just try to be the best possible you. There is not a single other person like you in the whole world. Don't make excuses. Prepare and do what you've got to do. If you didn't prepare, say so, apologize, take the consequences, and do better next time.

A calm spirit. Try to take time to be silent and to listen to your inner self, where God lives. Be able to be alone without being lonely. Don't think you have to be *doing* something all the time—an addiction La La has struggled to break all my life. I know I need to withdraw into silence regularly to get and retain my bearings and to be a calmer person.

A loving spirit that wells up in wonder and laughter and newness your whole life because you know you are loved. You already have it. Nurture it. Love is the most important value in life. Love of God, of self, and of your neighbor as yourself.

P.S. I hope all of you will keep a diary or journal. You can tell it everything that you may not want to say to anyone else. Tell it when you are happy or sad. Tell it about your friends and your feelings and your dreams and about your day. You forget so much of what goes on in your life and will be so surprised and pleased to see how you have grown and changed and not changed. I kept one for many years and I do now. Wish I'd done it all the time.

A Letter to Our Leaders About America's Sixth Child and the Cradle to Prison Pipeline Crisis

America is going to hell if we don't use her vast resources to end poverty and make it possible for all of God's children to have the basic necessities of life.

——MARTIN LUTHER KING JR.

They have become great and rich
They have grown fat and sleek . . .
They judge not with justice
The cause of their fatherless
They do not defend the rights of the needy.

——JEREMIAH 5:27–28

Once to every man and nation comes the
  moment to decide,
In the strife of Truth with Falsehood for
  the good or evil side;
Some great Cause, God's New Messiah,
  offering each the bloom or blight,

Parts the goats upon the left hand, and
   the sheep upon the right,
And the choice goes by forever 'twixt that
   darkness and that light.

—JAMES RUSSELL LOWELL

GREENLESS CHILD

I watched her go uncelebrated into the second grade,
A greenless child,
Gray among the orange and yellow,
Attached too much to corners and to other people's sunshine.
She colors the rainbow brown
And leaves balloons unopened in their packages.
Oh, who will touch this greenless child?
Who will plant alleluias in her heart
And send her dancing into all the colors of God?
Or will she be left like an unwrapped package on the kitchen table—
Too dull for anyone to take the trouble?
Does God think we're her keeper?

—ANN WEEMS

AMERICA'S SIXTH CHILD

Imagine God visiting our very wealthy family blessed with six children. Five of them have enough to eat and comfortable warm rooms in which to sleep. One does not. She is often hungry and cold. On some nights, she has to sleep on the streets or in a shelter and even be taken away from her neglectful family and placed in foster care or group homes with strangers.

Imagine this rich family giving five of its children nourishing meals three times a day, snacks to fuel boundless energy, but sending the sixth child from the table and to school hungry, with only one or two meals and never the dessert the other children enjoy.

Imagine this very wealthy family making sure five of its children get all of their shots, regular health checkups before they get sick, and immediate access to health care when illness strikes but ignoring the sixth child, who is plagued by chronic respiratory infections and painful toothaches, which sometimes abscess and kill for lack of a doctor or a dentist.

Imagine this family sending five of their children to good stimulating preschools and making sure they have music and swimming lessons after school but sending the sixth child to unsafe daycare with untrained caregivers responsible for too many children or leaving her occasionally with an accommodating relative or neighbor or older sibling or alone.

Imagine five of the children living in homes with books in families able to read to most of their children every night, but leaving the other child unread to, untalked and unsung to, unhugged, or propped before a television screen or video game that feeds him violence and sex and racially and gender-charged messages, intellectual pablum, interrupted only by ceaseless ads for material things beyond the child's grasp.

Imagine this family sending some of their children to high-quality schools in safe neighborhoods with enough books and computers and laboratories and science equipment and well-prepared teachers and sending the sixth child to a crumbling school building with peeling ceilings and leaks and lead in the paint and asbestos and old, old books—and not enough of them—and teachers untrained in the subjects they teach and with low expectations that all children can learn, especially the sixth child.

Imagine most of the family's children being excited about learning, and looking forward to finishing high school, going to college, and getting a job, and the sixth child falling further and further behind grade level, not being able to read, wanting to drop out of school, and being suspended and expelled at younger and younger ages, because no one has taught him to read and compute or diagnosed his attention deficit disorder or treated his health and mental health problems and helped him keep up with his peers.

Imagine five of the children engaged in sports and music and arts, in after-school and summer camps, and in enrichment programs, and the sixth child hanging out with peers or going home alone because Mom and Dad are working, in prison, or have run away from their parenting responsibilities and escaped in drugs and alcohol, leaving him alone or on the streets during idle nonschool hours and weeks and months, at risk of being sucked into illegal activities and the prison pipeline or killed in our gun-saturated nation.

This is our American family today, where one in six of our children lives in poverty in the richest nation on earth, more than 40 percent in extreme poverty. It is not a stable, healthy, economically sensible, or just family. Our failure to invest in all our children before they get sick, or drop out of school and get into trouble is morally indefensible and extremely costly. Every year that we let 13 million children live in poverty costs $500 billion in lost productivity, and cost of crime and health. You cannot hurt others, especially children, without consequences.

Contrary to popular stereotypes, America's sixth child is more than twice as likely to live in a working family than to be on welfare, is more likely to be white than black or Latino, and is more likely to live in a rural or suburban area than in an inner city. However, black and Hispanic children are at far greater risk of being poor and of entering the Cradle to Prison Pipeline. The most dangerous place for a child to try to grow up in America today is at the intersection of race and poverty. Racial disparities still permeate all the major American institutions that shape the life chances of millions of children. Undergirded by poverty, those disparities are putting countless children at risk of incarceration and funneling hundreds of thousands of them every year into a pipeline to prison, derailing their chances for reaching successful adulthood.

Incarceration is becoming the new American slavery and poor children of color are the fodder. As leaders you must see, understand, and sound the alarm about this threat to American unity and community, act to stop the growing criminalization of children at younger and younger ages, and tackle the unjust treatment of minority youths and adults in the juvenile and adult criminal justice systems with urgency and persistence. The failure to act now will reverse the hard-earned racial and social progress Dr. King and so many others died and sacrificed for and weaken our future capacity to lead. All leaders in all sectors must call for investment in all children from birth through their successful transition to adulthood, remembering Frederick Douglass's correct observation that "it is easier to build strong children than to repair broken men."

So many poor babies in rich America enter the world with multiple strikes against them: born without prenatal care, at low birthweight, and to a teen, poor, and poorly educated single mother and absent father. At crucial points in their development after birth until adulthood, more risks pile on, making a successful transition to productive adulthood significantly less likely and involvement in the criminal justice system significantly more likely. Since children of color always have been disproportionately poor, their odds of incarceration as adults greatly exceed that of white children. Black children are more than three times as likely as white children to be poor, and are almost six times as likely as white children to be incarcerated.

A poor black boy born in 2001 has a one in three chance of going to prison in his lifetime; a Latino boy a one in six chance; a black girl a one in seventeen chance; a white boy a one in seventeen chance; a Latina girl a one in forty-five chance and a white girl a one in one hundred and eleven chance.

The past continues to strangle the present and the future. Children with an incarcerated parent are more likely to become incarcerated. Black children are nearly nine times and Latino children are three times as likely as white children to have an incarcerated parent. Blacks constitute one third and Latinos one fifth of our imprisoned population. One in three black men, 20 to 29 years old, is under correctional supervision or control. Of the 2.3 million in jail or prison, 64 percent are minority. Of the 4.2 million persons on probation, 45 percent are minority; of the 800,000 on parole, 59 percent are minority. Unjust drug sentencing policies have greatly escalated the incarceration of minority adults and youth.

These numbers are a black and Latino community tragedy and a national catastrophe. They are ripping apart millions of families, stripping away the right to vote for many, and blocking the chance to get a job to support a family. They decrease public security as more and more prisoners reenter society without the means to legally support themselves, and drain taxpayer dollars as increasing billions are spent on massive incarceration of young and old. We need to change course.

Child poverty and neglect, racial disparities in systems that serve children, and the Cradle to Prison Pipeline are not acts of God. They are America's immoral political and economic choices that can and must be changed with strong political, corporate, and community leadership. No single sector or group can solve these child- and nation-threatening crises alone but all of us can together. As leaders, you must call us to the table and use your bully pulpits to replace our current paradigm of punishment as a first resort with a paradigm of prevention and early intervention. It will save lives, save families, save taxpayer money, and save our nation's aspiration to be a fair society.

If called to account today, America would not pass the test of the prophets, the Gospels, and all great faiths. Christians who profess to believe that God entered human history as a poor vulnerable baby, and that each man, woman, and child is created in God's own image, need to act on that faith. The Jewish Midrash says God agreed to give the people of Israel the Torah only after they offered their children as guarantors, deeming neither their prophets nor elders sufficient. It is time to heed the prophets' call for justice for the orphans and the weak. America's Declaration of Independence says, "We hold these truths to be self-evident, that all men are created equal, and are endowed by their creator with certain inalienable rights." After more than two centuries, it is time to make those truths evident in the lives of poor children of color and to close our intolerable national hypocrisy gap. America's sixth child is waiting for you and all of us to welcome them into their rich land and show the world whether democratic capitalism is an oxymoron or can work. Our national creed demands that we end child poverty, neglect, and abuse *now*. All great faiths, simple human decency, and moral redemption demand it. Common sense and self-interest require it. And our credibility in the world we seek to lead compels it.

Ending child poverty is not only an urgent moral necessity, it is economically beneficial. Dr. Robert M. Solow, M.I.T. Nobel Laureate in Economics, wrote in *Wasting America's Future* that "ending child poverty is, at the very least, highly affordable. More likely it is a gain to the economy, and the businesses, taxpayers, and citizens within." A healthy Social Security and Medicare system for our increasing elderly population need as many productive workers as possible to support them. We can ill afford to let millions of our children grow up poor, in poor health, uneducated, and as dependent rather than productive citizens.

What then can leaders do to help build our spiritual and political will to help our nation pass the test of the God of history and better prepare for America's future? What steps can you take to heed Dr. King's warning not to let our wealth become our destruction but our salvation by helping the poor Lazaruses languishing at our gates? How can you help us seize the enormous opportunity to use our blessings to bless all the children entrusted to our care and rekindle America's dimming dream?

A NINE-STEP PROGRAM FOR AMERICA'S LEADERS TO END CHILD POVERTY AND THE CRADLE TO PRISON PIPELINE CRISIS

Step one: *Call us to be our best selves. Lead us in building a united and compassionate national house where the deep divides between rich and poor, white and nonwhite, men and women, and imprisoned and free are bridged.* Despite huge strides over the past four decades, the nation's racial and economic progress is stalling and threatening to reverse. Get us on the right track again by leading us forward and not backward. Reset our nation's priorities that have created the greatest gap between rich and poor in our history by committing to investing in the future of every child from birth through college and productive adulthood. Lead us away from false either-ors between personal, family, community, and societal responsibility for children and from simplistic solutions that don't address these complex but solvable problems. Since all of us are responsible for ensuring our nation's future, call us to work together and to put the child's healthy development at the center of our decision-making. If the child is safe, all of us are.

Step two: *Commit in 2009 to end indefensible and preventable child poverty by 2015—the date of the United Nations Millennium Development Goals for developing nations—and the racial disparities suffered by millions of black, Latino, and Native American children who are disproportionately poor in the richest nation on earth.* No other industrialized nation permits the high rates of child poverty we do. Benjamin Franklin said that the best family policy is a good job. Every American family should have an adequate income based primarily on work and a decent safety net for anyone unable to work. Everyone must be able to live in healthy, safe, job-rich communities with affordable housing. And don't tell us we lack the money to end child poverty. Every child could be lifted out of poverty for less than nine months of the tax cuts for the top 1 percent and four months of the Iraq War. The irresponsible giveaways to our richest 300,000 Americans need to be reinvested in saving the futures of 13 million poor children. We do not have a money problem; we have a values and priorities problem.

Our new president and Congress must propose and fight hard for tax relief for low- and moderate-income families,

including a fully refundable child tax credit, which would lift
2.1 million children from poverty, and expansion of the Earned
Income Tax Credit (EITC), which could lift millions more
from poverty. Increasing the minimum wage to half the average
wage would help 1.7 million people leave poverty; expanding
federal child care support to families earning 200 percent or
below the federal poverty level would lift 2.7 million children
and parents from poverty; and raising food stamp participation
to 85 percent would reduce the poverty of 1.4 million people,
according to the Center for American Progress. We know what
to do; we just need your leadership to get it done.

Educate us about who the poor are and show us that they are
like the rest of us. Help our nation remove its psychological
cataracts and dispel the myths we hear so often about the causes
and consequences of child poverty: (1) *"It costs too much to eliminate
child poverty."* Although the cost to America's soul and ideals of not
eliminating child poverty is beyond measure, it costs more economically *not* to eliminate poverty, as a recent Center for American Progress (CAP) report and two previous CDF reports on *The
Cost of Child Poverty* and *Wasting America's Future*, show. We cannot
afford to throw away $500 billion in annual productivity by
keeping 13 million children poor. (2) *"It is not the right time."* It is
always the right time to do right by children and the poor. During
economic downturns, children should not be the first to suffer
huge budget cuts or be the last to benefit during economic up-
turns. President Reagan was fond of saying that we fought a war
on poverty and poverty won. Well, the war on poverty was a brief
scrimmage, not a war. In 1968, when Dr. King called for a Poor
People's Campaign, we were investing forty times less in the
Office of Economic Opportunity to fight the war on poverty than
in the war in Vietnam and other military spending. (3) *"Nothing*

works." Many things work; we simply do not provide them to all eligibles. Only 3 percent of eligible children get Early Head Start; less than two thirds of eligible children get regular Head Start; only 87 percent of children eligible for food stamps and 12 percent of children eligible for summer food programs get them. About 6 million children eligible for the State Children's Health Insurance Program (SCHIP) and Medicaid health services don't receive them. Let's make sure that every eligible child gets demonstrably successful programs through simplified bureaucracy better outreach, and adequate funding. (4) *"Children are not my responsibility. They are their parents' responsibility."* Parents should do everything they can to raise and support their children, but if they work and play by the rules and still cannot make ends meet and private sector policies do not protect them, government must. When jobs are exported abroad or disappear during recession, children should not suffer. No child should be punished for parents they did not choose. (5) *"The poor should not have babies they cannot support."* No one should have children they can't support emotionally as well as financially. But who among us has the right to decide who should bear a child or blame and punish children for their parents' actions? We need to help rather than judge or blame or punish the poor or non-poor who neglect their children. (6) *"It's class warfare to talk about redistributing income to the poor."* No one should contend this in light of governmental policies that historically have provided and continue to provide tax breaks and subsidies to the richest and most powerful corporations and individuals. Who should have first call on government resources—those who need most or those who have most? How can it be fair that in 2003, forty-six companies paid no federal income taxes while reporting combined profits of $42.6 billion and collectively receiving tax *rebates* totaling $5.4 billion?

Step three: *Immediately ensure **every** child a healthy start through guaranteed comprehensive health and mental health coverage and prenatal care wherever they live in America.* Senior citizens have Medicare and children should be guaranteed similar health protection across all fifty states. As an interim step in 2009, if universal coverage is not immediately possible, CDF has developed the All Healthy Children Act to cover *all* pregnant mothers and children, simplify the two current child health bureaucracies (Medicaid and SCHIP), and ensure a guaranteed national benefit package to all children. There should no longer be fifty different state determinations of a child's worth and health outcomes or a grossly inadequate child health and mental health care non-system that feeds children into the Cradle to Prison Pipeline. So many low birthweight babies are at risk for future health and learning difficulties. Undiagnosed, untreated, and poorly managed health and mental health problems increase a child's chances of falling behind in school or having disciplinary problems, and decrease a child's chances of succeeding in and out of school. Our woefully inadequate mental health care system causes the inappropriate incarceration of thousands of children and youth in costly juvenile detention facilities solely because community mental health services are unavailable. Children who go into the juvenile justice system are at greater risk for entering the adult criminal justice system.

Step four: *Ensure quality parent-child home visiting programs, and quality Early Head Start, Head Start, child care, and preschool to get every child ready for school.* Investing in high-quality early childhood care and development programs for disadvantaged children yields high returns that extend beyond success in school into adulthood. Children who participated in such programs were more likely to be in better health, to have completed higher levels of education, to have higher earnings, to be married or in stable relationships, and to be less likely to commit a crime or be incarcerated. Since education is a key determinant of future success, and because brain development is greatest in the first three years of life, early childhood investment pays big dividends later.

Step five: *Dramatically decrease the number of children who enter the child welfare system.* A poor child is twenty-two times more likely to be neglected and abused and to face removal from home than a non-poor child. The overburdened and underfinanced child welfare system is a major feeder system into the Cradle to Prison Pipeline and perpetuator of racial disparities. Black children represent 16 percent of the child population but 32 percent of the foster care population. Children who age out of foster care are less likely to graduate from high school or college and to experience more serious mental health problems than children generally; are less likely to receive adequate health and mental health care; are more likely to experience homelessness and to be involved in the criminal justice system. Increased support for the 4.5 million children living in grandparent-headed households and 1.5 million living with other relatives who are legal guardians is important, as are policies requiring notice to grandparents and kin before a child is placed in foster care and kinship navigator programs to link relative caregivers to services children need. Promoting safe permanent families for children at risk for out of home placement by redirecting federal child welfare funding toward prevention and improved treatment services for troubled families is essential. Measures to prevent teen pregnancy and to provide quality family and community support programs for parents are also important. Teen birth rates fell by 34 percent between 1991 and 2005, but still a baby is born to a teen mother every minute. The best contraceptive is hope. Hope comes from a sense of a positive future. The two largest predictors of who will become a teen parent are poverty and basic skills level. Ending child and family poverty and providing every child a quality education are crucial.

Step six: *Make sure every child can read by fourth grade and can graduate from high school able to succeed in college, at work, and in life.* Not being able to read is a sentence to social and economic death. A high school diploma is the best ticket out of poverty, although the goal post for getting a stable foothold in our economy today has moved beyond a high school to a college diploma. Greater education investment with greater accountability must become a reality. President Bush said he was going to be the education president, but after he took office, he invested $50 billion more in tax cuts for the richest 1 percent and $330 billion more on the war in Iraq than in elementary and secondary education. Adequate federal, state, and local resources are needed to ensure smaller class sizes and higher teacher quality, to fund universal high-quality preschool education, and to repair crumbling schools. You must encourage and provide incentives for more young people, especially more minority youths, to see teaching and educational administration as urgent callings. Failing schools are a major feeder system of poor children into the prison pipeline and incarceration.

Step seven: *We must link all children to a permanent, caring family member or adult mentor who can keep them on track and get them back on track if and when they stray.* The fabric of community must be rewoven to catch falling children until our torn family fabric can be repaired. We must bring to scale promising practices that engage and enrich children during out-of-school time. Children spend much more time out of school than in school and need positive alternatives to the streets and television. Every mayor and county supervisor needs to implement summer feeding programs, which are 100 percent federally funded, in their city, town, and county. They create jobs, keep children from going hungry, and can provide the foundation for high-quality summer enrichment programs to help disadvantaged children retain and expand regular school-year learning gains.

Step eight: *Reform the juvenile justice system, a major feeder system into the prison pipeline that disproportionately confines minority youth.* Black juveniles are four times as likely and Latino youths are twice as likely as their white peers to be incarcerated, and black youths are almost five times as likely and Latino youths are twice as likely to be incarcerated as white youths for comparable drug offenses. One of the most successful examples of rehabilitating children in youth detention is the "Missouri Miracle," which reduced recidivism to 7 percent in fiscal year 2005 and brought significant cost savings to the state. Missouri has a full range of juvenile programs, from day treatment to community-based facilities to secure detention. In 2005, the average daily cost for a youth in a community-based facility was $112.62 (about $41,000 a year), and $156.63 per day (about $57,000 a year) for secure care. Some states spend between $100,000 and $200,000 per year for a single bed in a youth correction facility. Children should not be detained in adult jails and vigilant federal, state, and local oversight must stop widespread abusive practices in the juvenile justice system across the country.

Step nine: *Confront America's deadly, historic romance with guns and violence and stress nonviolent values and conflict resolution in all aspects of American life.* I applaud the leadership of the mayors to curb gun violence and illegal guns. Measures requiring background checks for individual purchasers of guns from gun shows and on the Internet, and the regulation of guns as a consumer product are long overdue. Leaders must speak out against excessive violence in our cultural programming and find ways to encourage greater emphasis on conflict resolution in our schools and congregations as steps toward breaking our cultural addiction to violence.

The poverty and racial inequities funneling millions of our children and youth into the prison pipeline must become the top domestic priority for all our leaders and the entire nation for the next decade. Being the world's leading jailer is hardly a distinction to be proud of. We cannot imprison our way out of injustice and inequality. As leaders you must stop sending our children on dead-end paths in life.

In 1965, poor Mississippi sharecroppers Mae Bertha and Matthew Carter wanted a better life for their seven younger children and knew this required a good education. They challenged the state of Mississippi's sham "freedom of choice" desegregation plans by applying to enroll their children in the "white" Drew, Sunflower County, Mississippi, public schools, home of powerful segregationist Senator Jim Eastland. I was privileged to be their attorney and watched with awe and humility as their family courageously withstood violence, eviction, daily harassment, and abuse. The younger Carter children, with their parents' unwavering love and support, weathered the daily cruelties in their school and community, graduated from high school and college, and became professionals contributing much to our nation. Connie Curry describes the heroic Carter family struggles in an inspiring book, *Silver Rights*. When Connie told me that Miz Mae Bertha's grandson, Lorenzo, was in prison in Parchman, Mississippi, it reignited my determination to sound the alarm against the growing resegregation, incarceration, and miseducation of black children and youth, especially young black males, that threatens to undo the hard-earned racial and social progress of the Civil Rights Movement, destroy the black family, disempower the black community, undermine our nation's future, and indelibly stain our pretensions to be a fair society.

Dr. Jonas Salk wrote in 1984 that "the brontosaurus became extinct, but it wasn't its fault, so to speak. If we become extinct, it will be our fault.... In order to survive, man has to evolve. And to evolve, we need a new kind of thinking and a new kind of behavior, a new ethic and a new morality. It will be that of the evolution of everyone rather than the survival of the fittest. In terms of evolutionary behavior, that means choosing at each moment to adopt the attitudes and values—cooperation, caring, loving, forgiving—that are absolutely essential if we are not to destroy ourselves. It's not easy, but is worth every difficulty. There is nothing mushy, vague, or soft-headed about loving and forgiving. In fact, the end result would be to release the power in the nucleus of each individual—a power much greater in its positive effects than atomic power in its negative."

If leaders love our country enough to protect all of our children, maybe God will forgive us for the suffering we had the means but not the will to stop—until now.

IS THIS A COUNTRY LIVING ITS CREED
AND PREPARING FOR THE FUTURE?

How America Ranks Among Industrialized
Countries in Investing In and Protecting Children

- 1st in gross domestic product
- 1st in number of billionaires in the world
- 1st in number of persons incarcerated

◄ 1st in health expenditures

◄ 1st in military technology

◄ 1st in defense expenditures

◄ 1st in military weapons exports

◄ 22nd in low birth weight rates

◄ 25th in infant mortality rates

◄ High in relative child poverty

◄ High in the gap between the rich and the poor

◄ High in teen (age 15 to 19) birthrates

◄ Last in protecting children against gun violence

◄ The United States of America and Somalia (which has no legally constituted government) are the only two United Nations members that have failed to ratify the U.N. Convention on the Rights of the Child.

ARE OUR CHILDREN READY TO COMPETE WITH THEIR PEERS IN CHINA, INDIA, JAPAN, AND ELSEWHERE?

Percent of 12th grade public school students *not* reading at grade level

Total, all races	65
White, non-Hispanic	57
Black	84
Hispanic	80

American Indian   74
Asian   64

Percent of 12th grade public school students not doing math at grade level

Total, all races   77
White, non-Hispanic   71
Black   94
Hispanic   92
American Indian   94
Asian   64

IF WE COMPARE JUST BLACK CHILD WELL-BEING
TO CHILDREN IN OTHER NATIONS:

⊰ 62 nations have lower infant mortality rates including Sri Lanka.

⊰ Over 100 nations have lower low birth weight births including Algeria, Botswana, and Panama.

⊰ Black women in the U.S. are more likely to die from complications of pregnancy or childbirth than women in Turkmenistan.

A Letter to Citizens–the Creators of Leaders and Movements

A CITIZEN'S PRAYER FOR FAIRNESS

O God, I am not smart enough to debate monetary, fiscal, or budget policy with the Federal Reserve, the Treasury, or the Congressional Budget Office. But I am a citizen and I know injustice when I see it. I know you told us when we give to the poor we lend to You. So when we take from the poor we steal from You.

Help me to stand up courageously against unjust tax and budget policies at every level of government that increase benefits for those who have much and decrease benefits for those who have little. Help me to stand up for political choices that close the gap between the rich and the poor and to stand up against choices which widen that gap.

Help me try to do what You would do.

A PRAYER FOR PERSEVERANCE AND COURAGE

O God
Grant us creative patience
to persist until we see what the end may be
Keep us from giving up just because the way is hard and uncertain
Help us never to cease trying to get children their fair share of concern in our
unheeding world because they are Your children.

God, help us to stand true to You whether others honor or despise us, criticize or
commend us.

What kind of people do we Americans seek to be in the twenty-first century? What kind of people do we want our children to be? What kind of choices and sacrifices are we prepared to make to realize a more just, compassionate, and less violent society and world—one safe and fit for every child?

A thousand years ago, the United States was not even a dream. Copernicus and Galileo had not told us the earth was round or that it revolved around the sun. Gutenberg's Bible had not been printed, Wycliffe had not translated it into English, and Martin Luther had not tacked his ninety-five theses on the church door. The Magna Carta did not exist, Chaucer's and Shakespeare's tales had not been spun, and the miraculous music of Bach, Beethoven, Mozart, and the Negro slaves in America had not been created to inspire and soothe our spirits. Many European serfs struggled in bondage while many African and Asian empires flourished in independence. Native Americans peopled America's soil free of slavery's blight, and Hitler's Holocaust had yet to show the depths human evil can reach when good women and men remain silent or indifferent.

A hundred or a thousand years from now, will civilization and humankind remain? Will America's dream be alive, be remembered, and be *worth* remembering? Will the United States be a blip or a beacon in history? Can our founding principle "that all men are created equal" and "are endowed by their Creator with certain inalienable rights" withstand the test of time, the tempests of politics and greed, and become deed and not just creed for every man, woman, and child? Is America's dream big enough for every second child who is female, every fifth child who is Latino, every sixth child who is poor, every sixth child who is black, and every seventh child who is mentally or physically challenged? And is our dream big enough to share with the 2.6 billion people worldwide who live in poverty, including the more than 10 million mothers, babies, and young children who die each year before age five, mainly from pregnancy, childbirth, and poverty related causes?

A churning new world order is being born that is affecting every citizen and human on Earth. Changing rules of doing global business are creating important new questions, challenges, and opportunities. Who will gain and who will be left behind? Will the chances of the poor, women, and children at home and around the world be enhanced or exploited? Will powerful corporate interests eviscerate or respect democratic nation-state decision-making processes? Will multinational conglomerates be accountable to or run roughshod over governments, communities, and citizens here at home and abroad in pursuit of quicker and bigger profits? Will the changing nature of work and the demands of the new economy strengthen or weaken already frayed family and community bonds and job

security? Will cultural homogenization and corporate brand-
ing contribute to or detract from the rich diversity of our nation's and world's peoples?

How can we close the spiraling divides between the rich and
the poor? And how can our warring ways be curbed and trans-
formed in a world teetering on the brink of nuclear suicide so
that our children can feel safe and hopeful again and trust adults
to protect them and their futures. "Sometimes," an eleven-year-old
wrote, "it occurs to me that I might not ever grow up."

If I could be granted only one wish and pass only one universal law, I would dismantle the arsenals of nuclear and conventional weapons of death in the world, produce no more, and
invest the trillions of saved resources in tools of life for the poor,
hungry, homeless, sick, and uneducated children and people on
God's earth. As citizens, we must make our nation take the lead
in reversing the arms race.

The U.S. has exerted and continues to wield disproportionate global influence as sole remaining "superpower." But our
moral authority, economic capacity, and ability to lead will continue to wane unless we get our house in order, practice our es-
poused values of freedom and justice, repair our crumbling
economy, and create the public education systems needed to prepare our children and country to compete in the years ahead.

What can citizens do to help our nation maintain its moral
authenticity and leadership? I hope we will demand that our
leaders:

*First: Make a significant down payment on universal health care
for all in 2009 by immediately providing all children and pregnant women with health coverage and commit to ending poverty.*
These would be powerful steps toward ending the Cradle to

Prison Pipeline. Most of the poor work, play by the rules, but cannot earn enough to make ends meet, get health care, or afford child care. Tax relief for the working poor and middle class must replace tax giveaways for the wealthiest; and safety net investments for those unable to work must be assured. We have millions more poor Americans in 2008 than in 1968 when Dr. King died calling for a poor people's campaign, although our GDP is three times richer.

Second: We must be vigilant and make sure we do not repeat the mistakes of the past. Our history of slavery and racial segregation teach that just as racial apartheid returned in an earlier era after our first bloody Civil War, it can happen again unless we are vigilant and address its reincarnation under new guises. Incarceration is becoming the new slavery. Millions of children are at risk of a Cradle to Prison Pipeline at birth. Its feeder systems—poverty and racism, failing families, schools, child welfare, and justice systems—must be addressed. If we are to assure a more just America, citizens must inform themselves about the causes driving incarceration and insist that political, economic, and community leaders in every sector reroute children to healthy adulthood. A paradigm of prevention and early intervention must replace punishment as a first resort.

Third: Understand that citizens must organize and make leaders lead. A lot of people are waiting for Dr. King to return or for a new charismatic leader to emerge to save us. But he's not coming back and no single leader can save us. We're it. A statement attributed to Gandhi that says: "There go my people; I must run to catch up with them for I am their leader," makes the point. In David Garrow's book, *Bearing the Cross*, Ella Baker, a crucial role model for me and hundreds of young people in the sit-in movement—who helped form SNCC, the Student Nonviolent Coordinating Committee, in Raleigh, North Carolina, at her alma mater Shaw University in April 1960—said, "The central fact of Martin Luther King's life which he realized from December 5 in Montgomery until April 4 in Memphis was that: 'The movement made Martin rather than Martin making the movement.'" Diane Nash, the Nashville, Tennessee, student sit-in leader, told Garrow: "If people think it was Martin Luther King's movement, then today they—young people—are more likely to say, 'gosh, I wish we had a Martin Luther King here today to lead us.' ... If people knew how that movement started, then the question they would ask themselves is, 'what can I do?'"

That's the question every woman, man, and child in America must ask ourselves today. Movements make leaders; leaders don't make movements. The people of Montgomery, Alabama, had been seething for years about their unjust treatment on the city's public buses. Mrs. Rosa Parks was the eventual trigger for a community-wide response, which propelled Dr. King, a reluctant prophet, into leadership. But many Montgomery citizens, including Jo Anne Robinson of the Women's Political Caucus and E. B. Nixon, head of the NAACP, were creating the community infrastructure and awaiting the right spark to create a great conflagration. When it came, it ignited the movement, which changed not only Montgomery but all of America.

Fourth: Citizens must be firemen—vigilant and courageous in speaking truth about our nation's failings. Near the end of his life, Dr. King was deeply discouraged about the ability of our economic system as it currently operated to confront the deep structural ills of the racism, excessive materialism, poverty, and militarism he warned could lead to our downfall. As he struggled to build support for the Poor People's Campaign to end poverty for white, black, Hispanic, and Native and Asian Americans (believing always that helping the black poor would help all the poor and all Americans), he confided to friends, "We have fought hard and long for integration, as I believe we should have, and I know that we will win. But I've come to believe we're integrating into a burning house.... I'm afraid that America may be losing what moral vision she may have had.... And I'm afraid that even as we integrate, we are walking into a place that does not understand that this nation needs to be deeply concerned with the plight of the poor and disenfranchised. Until we commit ourselves to ensuring that the underclass is given justice and opportunity, we will continue to perpetuate the anger and violence that tears at the soul of this nation." Asked what one should do, he responded, "I think we are just going to have to become firemen."

Fifth: Vote for children and monitor how those you vote for protect children. Find out how well your members of Congress are standing up for children at www.cdfactioncouncil.org. Be a good citizen-mentor for your children and grandchildren. Every parent and grandparent, aunt and uncle should get out and vote and take your child, grandchild, niece, nephew, or a neighbor's child with you. Let's teach children by example the importance of voting in a democracy. Women who waited 143 years for the right to exercise our citizenship and blacks who gained the franchise only after long decades of struggle have a special responsibility to honor the sacrificial efforts of our ancestors. That only 65.4 percent of women and 60 percent of blacks and only 46.7 percent of 24.9 million eligible young voters ages eighteen to twenty-four (who did not have to wait or struggle at all) voted in the 2004 election is a wasted opportunity. How exciting to see the high voter turnout in the primaries this year and the excitement of all these groups about the possibility of change.

Sixth: Be thermostat citizens who work to change the political climate. The parents, children, and pioneer lawyers whose courage led to *Brown v. Board of Education* did not wait for government to act: they stood up and pushed government for what their children—and our country—needed. They were what Dr. King called thermostat leaders who changed the climate rather than thermometer leaders who held up their fingers to test and submit to the prevailing political temperature. Child advocates and faith, community, and young leaders must stand up and challenge unjust budget priorities and make our nation stand up for children who are our collective future. So let us begin. We don't have to be Dr. King or Mother Teresa. We just have to care and commit to serving and working with others to save our children, each of us doing what we can.

I CARE AND AM WILLING TO SERVE AND STAND WITH
OTHERS TO SAVE OUR CHILDREN AND NATION

Lord I cannot preach like Martin Luther King Jr.
or turn a poetic phrase like Maya Angelou or Robert Frost
but I care and am willing to serve and stand with others for children.

I do not have Harriet Tubman's courage
or Indira Gandhi's and Eleanor Roosevelt's political skills
but I care and am willing to serve and stand with others for children.

I cannot sing like Fannie Lou Hamer or Aretha Franklin
or organize like Ella Baker and Bayard Rustin
but I care and am willing to serve and stand with others for children.

I am not holy like Archbishop Tutu, forgiving like President
Mandela, or disciplined like Mahatma Gandhi
but I care and am willing to serve and stand with others for children.

I am not brilliant like Dr. W.E.B. DuBois, Albert Einstein, or
Elizabeth Cady Stanton, or as eloquent as Sojourner Truth and
Booker T. Washington
but I care and am willing to serve and stand with others for children.

I have not Mother Teresa's or Dorothy Day's saintliness,
the Dalai Lama's or César Chávez's gentle tough spirits
but I care and am willing to serve and stand with others for children.

God, it is not as easy as the sixties
to frame an issue and forge a solution
but I care and am willing to serve and stand with others for children.

My mind and body are not so swift as in youth
and my energy comes in spurts
but I care and am willing to serve and stand with others for children.

I'm so young
nobody will listen
I'm not sure what to say or do
but I care and am willing to serve and stand with others for children.

I can't see or hear well
speak good English, stutter sometimes
and get real scared, standing up before others
but I care and am willing to serve and stand with others for children.

Lord, please use me as You will to save Your children today and
tomorrow and to build a nation and world where no child is left
behind and everyone feels welcome.

The Mother of All Issues–Pregnancy and Childbirth: A Letter to Mothers, Grandmothers, and All Women

Mothers. Grandmothers. Women.

We have so much work to do.

So many mothers and infant lives to save.

So many child dreams to realize and hopes to nourish and protect.

Our countries and a common world to change and such long distances to travel—from waging war to waging peace; from sickness and death to health; from doubt to faith in Creator's feminine spirit within

Let some of us—you and I—begin this minute on that journey

To speak for those unable to speak for themselves

To stand with those who cannot stand alone

To gather family and friends to stand with us.

Let us begin this day singing a new song for all our mothers and sisters and brothers and fathers and children around our world who are our own.

As a woman, I have no country. As a woman, I want no country. As a woman, my country is the whole world.

—VIRGINIA WOOLF

TELL ME WHERE TO BE BORN

People of the world, tell me where to be born.
If I were born in the land of "your interest" would you let me die?
People of the world, my name is Holocaust and I'm fifty plus years old.
My name is Sarajevo and I'm three years old.
My name is Bijac and I'm but a month old.
I have no name, I'm yet to be born.
People of the world, tell me where to be born, so you will not hate me one day, so you will not maim me one day, so you will not kill me one day.
People of the world, tell me where to be born.

—AVIDEH SHASHAANI

If the first woman God ever made was strong enough to turn the world upside down all alone, these women together ought to be able to turn it back, and get it right side up again.

—SOJOURNER TRUTH, SLAVE WOMAN WHO FOUGHT FOR WOMEN'S EQUALITY AND SLAVERY'S ABOLITION (*AIN'T I A WOMAN?*, 1857)

There is an African proverb that says "women hold up half the sky." Women constitute more than half the world's population, perform nearly two-thirds of its work, bear all of the babies, and have primary responsibility for raising the children who constitute 100 percent of the world's future. But women have not realized half of the world's potential, have not received half of the world's resources, or exercised half of the world's power. Women get less than half of the educational opportunities provided, and are the largest victims of war and poverty. Women and children make up the majority of the poor and the majority of the victims of domestic violence in the world. And we face an unparalleled death toll from a singular gift from which men are exempt: pregnancy and childbirth.

The single greatest preventable cause of death in today's world is pregnancy and childbirth. More than seven million mothers, stillborns, and newborns are lost each year, most unknown outside their families or villages. This is incomprehensible to me in a world that purports to be civilized. That's 20,000 human beings like you and me and our children every day; 833 an hour; 14 a minute; 1 every 4 seconds. Only cancer, for which there is no vaccine or cure, slightly exceeds this staggering death toll. It is more than three times the number of deaths from AIDS in 2007; more than four times the deaths from tuberculosis in 2006; and seven times the deaths from malaria in 2007.

By the end of 2005, 25 million people had died of AIDS since the pandemic's tragic onset around 1981. The estimated number of maternal, stillbirths, and newborn deaths surpasses this astronomical AIDS death toll every 3.4 years. Over a thirty-year period, pregnancy- and childbirth-related losses exceed all the casualties from all the wars in the twentieth century. Yet it goes on and on, largely invisible and in silence.

Imagine what we would think and do in the United States and in the world if we heard that every one of the 4.3 million infants expected to be born in the United States this year and most of next year were going to die before birth or in the first month of life along with 536,000 of their mothers. Or that the entire populations of Los Angeles or Chicago were going to disappear in a year. Imagine our reaction if we learned that all of Finland's or Ireland's people would die next year or that Great Britain's population would disappear in less than nine years unless we mobilized and acted together with urgency to save them from a largely preventable catastrophe.

It's time for the women of the world to stand up and say STOP to the massive, chronic, annual invisible genocide of mothers and babies. At the current rate of progress on the Millennium Development Goals related to maternal mortality and health, a majority of developing nations will not meet them. It is time for the women of the world to raise a ruckus!

Why is there such silence and failure to stop this relentless, largely preventable mother-infant tragedy?

Is it because we believe these stillbirths and dying infants and mothers of Sub-Saharan Africa and South Asia, where almost 90 percent of these deaths occur, don't threaten our personal lives or nations in any direct way? Is it because pregnancy and childbirth are not diseases we can catch? The United States has spent more than $6 billion since 2004 to prepare for a pandemic such as bird flu, which to date has killed 240 people. Why would equal or more attention and investment not be warranted in maternal and newborn health, since so many lives are at stake and we know what is needed to help save them?

Is it because some feel it's just poor mothers and babies of color cluttering what they consider our overpopulated earth? The maternal mortality gap between rich and poor nations is the greatest among all our glaring global inequities.

Is it because it's just mothers, who in some cultures are devalued and lack the most basic human rights and the power to protect and speak up for themselves and to choose whether and when to have children? In one meeting of the Global Women's Action Network for Children convened by CDF with women leaders from around the world a participant said that if a cow dies it is considered an economic tragedy; if a wife dies in childbirth, the husband just gets another one.

Is it because the controversies surrounding the 13 percent of maternal deaths from abortion cause the 87 percent from nonabortion causes to be ignored? Both sets of deaths might be prevented with skilled birth attendants, emergency obstetric care and the most basic health infrastructure and care privileged mothers like me take for granted. In Africa, less than 50 percent of births are attended by a skilled health worker. Fewer mothers have access to emergency obstetrics care.

Is it because privileged women have not been aware of this unspeakable death and suffering and so have not mobilized our voices to save and empower our less fortunate sisters and their babies? Shall we continue to let the lottery of birth dictate the life and death chances of millions of mothers and children in our resource-rich earth?

In the United States, 47 million people lack health insurance, including 9.4 million children, and 750,000 uninsured women give birth every year. We are the only industrialized nation that does not provide coverage for prenatal care for all mothers. The Congress and president refused to do so again in 2007 claiming no money. Yet the average cost in 2004 for providing prenatal care for each pregnant woman in our nation was $1,852 compared to the average $15,100 cost of intensive care for each low birth-weight baby requiring it. The United States ranks twenty-second in the percentage of low birth-weight babies and twenty-fifth in infant mortality rates among industrialized nations and these two health indicators for black children lag behind those in many developing nations. It is time for the United States to stop being an underdeveloped nation in the care and protection of the lives of mothers and children. What is our excuse?

In the poorest ten countries of the world mothers are 750 times as likely to die in pregnancy or childbirth as mothers in the richest ten industrialized countries. Using UNICEF's classification of regions, a mother in an industrialized country has a I in 8,000 lifetime risk of dying, in South Asia a I in 59 risk, and in Sub-Saharan Africa a I in 22 risk. A mother in Niger has a I in 7 risk and in Afghanistan a I in 8 risk compared to a mother in Ireland, who has a I in 47,600 risk, in Sweden a I in 17,400 risk, and in the United States a I in 4,800 risk. Ninety-nine percent of the 536,000 maternal deaths each year occur in developing countries: Sub-Saharan Africa and South Asia together account for 86 percent of global maternal deaths. India has the single largest number of maternal deaths of any nation (117,000); 2,380,000 of the 3 million stillbirths and almost 3 million of the 3.7 million newborns who die in the first twenty-eight days of life from pregnancy- and childbirth-related causes are in poor nations in these regions.

These deaths are compounded by the living hell of over 20 million women who survive childbirth each year but suffer life-long disabilities like fistula which often leave them shunned by family and community.

It's time for a new women's movement that cuts across race and class and faith and place to raise an irresistible voice to stop the dying of mothers and infants whose fates are inextricably intertwined. There is an urgent need for more vocal, independent, collaborative, and sustained advocacy between powerful, organized women leaders for women and children focused on specific goals. We must build stronger bridges between women in government and in civil society to protect mothers and children, to empower women and to build the political will to make the needs of women and children a top priority in the corridors of power. Eleanor Roosevelt believed that only powerful women would protect powerless women and that a woman's will is the strongest thing in the world. It's time for that women's will to forge a world fit and safe for every mother and child beginning with pregnancy and birth.

While great strides have been made in penetrating bastions of male privilege and power where the world's agenda and priorities are set, it is far, far from enough. We now have twenty-three women heading national governments, about 11 percent; five women currently hold U.S. cabinet positions; 23 percent of U.S. state legislators are women; and 26 percent of top leadership positions in the United Nations are held by women. In the United States in 2008, in a precedent-breaking year, a woman, Senator Hillary Rodham Clinton, was a leading contender for the Democratic presidential nomination. In 2007, we elected a woman Speaker of the House of Representatives, Nancy Pelosi, but the sixteen women members of the Senate and seventy of the House add up to only 16 percent of these powerful bodies. The United States' eight women governors constitute only 16 percent of the total.

Inequities against women and children in our world and in our own nation will not change unless and until a critical mass of women demand it. Children need their mothers. Families, communities, and national development need the survival, education, and leadership of women. Muhammad Yunus's microcredit and Rwanda's economic development experiences show that an investment in women yields greater positive family and community benefits. To write off and fail to educate and to use the enormous potential and talent of women anywhere, over one half of humanity, is to smite our global and national faces.

Just as the life and death chances of mothers and their children are inextricably intertwined, so are the life chances of mothers, infants, and girls inextricably connected to girls' education now and in the future. Our nations and the world have the capacity and responsibility to ensure all children—girls and boys—an education. It would cost less than what the United States is currently spending on the military in one week to provide the necessary level of support needed annually to educate the 72 million children not in school in our world, including 41 million girls. Based on UN Millennium Project estimates, the United States alone could finance such outlays for several years with the amount our country spends each year on the Iraq war. If our president and congressional leaders decided we couldn't do this alone, they could become the new global voice of conscience calling on other rich nations to tithe a fraction of all investments in weapons of death for tools of life.

If the women of America rekindle the extraordinary examples of our foremothers, we could—as we must—transform the values and priorities of our nation and, through it, the world. Women have always been the invisible backbone of transforming social movements and of anchor institutions in society: our families, congregations, schools, and communities. It took Mrs. Rosa Parks's sitting down to get the Montgomery community and Dr. King to stand up for justice. As honorary cochair of CDF's 1996 and 1997 Stand for Children Days, which built the grassroots movement to help enact the bipartisan Hatch-Kennedy State Children's Health Insurance Program (SCHIP), which provided health coverage to 6 million children, Mrs. Parks said, "If I could sit down for justice, you can stand up for children." Yes we can; we can unite to cover every single one of the 9.4 million uninsured children and all pregnant mothers in America and seek significantly increased and adequate budget investment in global maternal and child health to stop the annual deaths of more than 7 million mothers, stillborns, and newborns. It was Rachel Carson's breaking of the silence about the poisoning of the earth that catalyzed the current environmental movement. Nobel Peace Prize Laureate Jody Williams highlighted landmine safety and Kenyan Nobel Peace Prize Laureate Wangari Maathai brought the Green Belt movement to Africa. And that courageous symbol of freedom in Myanmar, Nobel Peace Prize Laureate Aung San Suu Kyi, shows what one woman can do to hold high the banner of hope and human rights.

Men have ruled the world for thousands of years and have brought us to the brink of nuclear holocaust and planetary destruction through militarism, global warming, and greed. They keep proclaiming allegiance to peace while preparing for war. Life on God's earth as we know it could end unless a dramatic change in values and priorities is demanded by a critical mass of the leaders and people of the world. Women must make this happen. September 11 and the AIDS pandemic show us that no nation's borders can protect any of us against nuclear disaster, terrorism, or disease. Massive and relentless mother and child deaths, which we have the capacity but not the will to stop, are an indelible spiritual stain on all humankind. But stop it we must and will—however long it takes. Join the Global Women's

Action Network for Children at gwanc@childrensdefense.org and let's get 7 million signatures on a petition to send to our U.S. president and world leaders to stop mothers and infants from dying now.

Let's get on with our movement—mothers and grandmothers and women of America and the world. Our mothers are dying and our children are crying.

A Letter to Dr. King

Martin Luther King Jr. is a voice, a vision, and a way. I call upon every Jew to hearken to his voice, to share his vision, to follow his way. The whole future of America will depend on the impact and influence of Dr. King.

—RABBI ABRAHAM JOSHUA HESCHEL INTRODUCING DR. KING TO
A RABBINICAL ASSEMBLY MARCH 25, 1968

We have assembled here . . . to give thanks to God that He gave to America, at this moment in history, Martin Luther King Jr. . . . and said to him: Martin Luther, speak to America about war and peace; about social justice and racial discrimination; about its obligation to the poor; and about non-violence as a way of perfecting social change in a world of brutality and war.

—MOREHOUSE COLLEGE PRESIDENT BENJAMIN E. MAYS'S
EULOGY OF APRIL 9, 1968

*A*lthough *you* have been gone forty years, you are with me every day. We have made much but far from enough progress in overcoming the tenacious national demons of racism, poverty, materialism, and militarism you repeatedly warned could destroy America and all of God's creation. So I wanted to write you a letter on what we have done and still have to do to realize your and America's dream. What a privilege it was to know, work with, and learn from you in the struggle to end racial segregation, discrimination, and poverty in our land.

Just as many Old and New Testament prophets in the Bible were rejected, scorned, and dishonored in their own land in their times, so were you by many when you walked among us. Now that you are dead, many Americans remember you warmly but have sanitized and trivialized your message and life. They remember Dr. King the great orator but not Dr. King the disturber of unjust peace. They applaud the Dr. King who opposed violence but not the Dr. King who called for massive nonviolent demonstrations to end war and poverty in our national and world house. They applaud your great 1963 "I Have a Dream" speech but ignore the promissory note still bouncing at America's bank of justice, waiting to be cashed by millions of poor and minority citizens. And they forget your repeated nightmares: the deaths of the four little girls in the Birmingham church and of three young civil rights workers in Mississippi's Freedom Summer and others across the South; the cries for Black Power begun during James Meredith's March Against Fear that you and others completed after he was shot; the growing violence in urban ghettos in southern and northern cities; the horrible, relentless violations of your human rights by FBI director J. Edgar Hoover; the storm of criticism that greeted your opposition to the Vietnam War, which you saw was stealing the hopes and lives of the poor at home and in that poor country; the outbreak of violence in a Memphis march you led in support of garbage workers; and the resistance to your call for a Poor People's Campaign to end the poverty then afflicting 25.4 million Americans, including 11 million children. We now have 36.5 million poor Americans including 13 million children although our gross domestic product (GDP) is three times larger than in 1968. And the gap between rich and poor in the United States is the highest ever recorded and higher than in every other wealthy industrialized nation.

But you struggled on as the civil rights leadership splintered, as white Americans tired of black demands, and as the country became preoccupied with Vietnam. I marveled every night during the long Meredith March from Memphis to Jackson at your patient discussions with Stokely Carmichael and Willie Ricks and other SNCC leaders who wanted to exclude whites from the movement and push you to endorse all necessary means for change, including violence. You listened as they vented their justified frustrations about the slow pace of racial progress and you tried to reason with them, repudiating their proposed "Black Power" slogan and strategies without repudiating them. You taught me and others of your followers how to parse out the good from the not so good, and to always seek common ground. And when you had no immediate solution you gave others the courtesy of a respectful hearing.

In the years between Montgomery and Memphis, you listened, learned, grew, and spoke the truth about what you discerned, and resisted those who sought to ghettoize your concern for social justice and peace. After your opposition to the Vietnam War provoked a firestorm of criticism by whites, blacks, friends, and foes, you correctly asserted that "nothing in the commandments you believed in set any national boundaries around the neighbors you were called to love." Black people told you to be quiet, not anger President Johnson and jeopardize his support for civil rights and antipoverty efforts. White people told you to be quiet because you were not an expert on foreign policy, as if black leaders and citizens had no stake in a war tearing our nation apart and taking disproportionate numbers of black children's lives, forgetting it was the "experts" that got us into this ill-fated war in the first place. Some contributors deserted you as you called not only for an end to the Vietnam War but for a fairer distribution of our country's vast resources between the rich and the poor. Why, they asked, were you pushing the nation to do more on the tail of the greatest civil rights strides ever and challenging a president who already had declared a war on poverty? You understood that our nation's ills went deeper and that our military budget of $80 billion and our Office of Economic Opportunity budget of less than $2 billion in 1968 to eliminate poverty was an unfair match.

Thanks to the tireless leadership of Coretta King and others over many years, our nation celebrates an official federal holiday in your honor every January. You are the only nonpresident so honored and the only person of color in our history. And after numerous stops and starts, plans to construct a memorial to you on our National Mall are moving closer to reality. It will be the first such memorial honoring not a president or war hero, but you—our citizen prophet of nonviolence and man of God who believed we *could* come together to build a beloved community. I am very proud that we Americans have come together to honor and celebrate you. I would be even prouder—and more sanguine about our future—if we committed to *following* you.

I caught a glimpse of your beloved community on the very beautiful morning of September 11, 2001, a day that changed America forever. It began gloriously for me in your hometown of Atlanta. I was attending the first Interfaith Alliance breakfast with several hundred Christian, Jewish, Muslim, Baha'i, Buddhist, Hindu, and political and community leaders of every color, to affirm our joint responsibility to ensure a safe and fit nation and world for all of God's children. I was moved to tears as the Harmony Children's Choir, who looked like a little United Nations, sang the anthem of our civil rights movement, "We Shall Overcome," more sweetly and convincingly than I had ever heard.

This taste of heaven on earth was shattered by hate and hell on earth as your close colleague and friend Andrew Young, who became Atlanta's mayor and United Nations ambassador after you died, met me at the door with the news of the terrorists' planes crashing into the World Trade Center and the Pentagon and of the unknown whereabouts of President Bush. I gasped aloud in horror at the world spinning out of control so suddenly, and experienced for the first time on our American mainland the terrors of war up close as many other nations already had experienced. Gone forever was our false sense of security and invulnerability that our military and economic might and political rhetoric had embedded in our collective psyches. My deepest initial fear was about the reaction of our leaders and the chance of a catastrophic third world war with nuclear weapons.

An irresistible urge to visit your grave site seized me. I wanted to tell you what had happened and to share the loving, hopeful vision of the morning darkened by the despair and death at the hands of faceless people whose names I did not know. Your prophetic warnings raced around my mind like the ticker tape at Rockefeller Center: "Our choice is no longer between violence and nonviolence but between nonviolence and nonexistence." I wondered what God was trying to teach us through this unspeakable tragedy. Could it be a chance to bring us closer to our world neighbors, or would it push us further apart? Surely the extraordinary courage, generosity, and sacrifice of so many trapped in or near the World Trade Center renewed our belief in human beings. One survivor of the twin towers attack said: "If you had seen what it was like in that stairway, you'd be proud. There was no gender, no race, no religion. It was everyone, unequivocally, helping each other." It was another unforgettable glimpse of your beloved community that terrible day in the very epicenter of catastrophe. Imagine what the world could become if we realized and practiced what this survivor felt, and what you repeatedly urged, in less catastrophic times?

I sat at your King Center grave site for a good spell, grateful to be near you, and then walked slowly up Auburn Avenue past Ebenezer Baptist Church, where you were ordained and preached with Daddy King. I wandered over to the front of your former Southern Christian Leadership Conference (SCLC) office, where we had discussed launching a Poor People's Campaign on a warm August day in 1967 to make visible the intolerable poverty of millions of white, black, brown, Asian, and Native American citizens denied a seat at America's table of plenty. We both knew that civil rights without economic rights did not add up to justice. As a civil rights lawyer in Mississippi, I knew my job was not finished when I won a school desegregation or public accommodation case and the next day my plaintiffs were thrown off their plantations, lost their jobs, had no way to feed their children, were shot at and their children harassed. I had to help them find a way to eat, a place to sleep, and protection for their children in hostile school environments if freedom was to be more than a hollow word. You knew that angry urban youths needed jobs, not sermons or scolding, and that hope with meat on its bones—jobs and education—was the only way to allay violence.

As you greeted me alone in your very modest office you appeared depressed, as you often were during the last two years of your life. I told you I'd just visited Robert Kennedy that morning at his Hickory Hill home in Virginia. I shared with him my deep frustration with the snail's pace in getting federal help to the hungry poor of the Mississippi Delta following his visit there in April 1967 when he had seen the empty cupboards of families with *no* income. When I told him I was stopping in Atlanta to see you on my way home to Jackson, he told me to tell you to "bring the poor to Washington." Your eyes and face lit up when I conveyed Robert Kennedy's message. You called me an angel and made a commitment on the spot to the idea and told Coretta that evening. She wrote, "He came home that night radiating his old enthusiasm and he said 'This is really it' . . . and I could see his excitement for the plan. . . . 'We should get people from all the poverty areas, from the South and from the North, people who don't have jobs or resources. . . . It must not be just black people, it must be all poor people.' . . . He realized that such a program would be a great change for the movement, which had always focused on Negro rights. Such a powerful coalition could really shake the established order and bring about needed structural changes to provide a better life for the poor."

Still in a somewhat surreal trance, I went across town to the chapel at Morehouse College, your alma mater, to read your words inscribed on your statue out front. Here is what you said:

Injustice anywhere is a threat to justice everywhere. We are caught in an inescapable network of mutuality, tied in a single garment of destiny. Whatever affects one directly affects all indirectly.

The richer we have become materially, the poorer we have become morally and spiritually. We have learned to fly the air like birds and swim the sea like fish, but we have not learned the simple art of living together as brothers.

⟋‿⟍

Nonviolence is a powerful and just weapon. It is a weapon unique in history, which cuts without wounding and enables the man who wields it. It is a sword that heals.

⟋‿⟍

If we are to have peace on earth, our loyalties must become ecumenical rather than sectional. Our loyalties must transcend our race, our tribe, our class, and our nation; and this means we must develop a world perspective. No individual can live alone; no nation can live alone, and as long as we try, the more we are going to have war in this world. Now the judgment of God is upon us, and we must either learn to live together as brothers or we are all going to perish together as fools.

I read your words aloud in my mind to the faceless terrorists and to our own leaders. I thought about your retelling of the story of the poor, sick beggar Lazarus and the rich man Dives in your last Sunday sermon at the Washington National Cathedral as you urged support for the Poor People's Campaign, and warned America that, like Dives, our wealth could be either our salvation or our downfall. And I remembered that you called your mother right before your death to give her your next Sunday sermon title: "Why America May Go to Hell." I also remembered your unflinching call at the Riverside Church for "a true revolution of values that will lay hands on the world order and say of war: This way of settling differences is not just. . . .

This business of burning human beings with napalm, of filling our nation's homes with orphans and widows, of injecting poisonous drugs of hate into the veins of people normally humane, of sending men home from dark and bloody battlefields physically handicapped and psychologically deranged, cannot be reconciled with wisdom, justice and love. A nation that continues year after year to spend more money on military defenses than on programs of social uplift is approaching spiritual death.... We must with positive action seek to remove those conditions of poverty, insecurity and injustice which are the fertile soil in which the seed of communism grows and develops," and in my mind I substituted the word *terrorism* for *communism*.

Your words strengthened my resolve to carry on your struggle to build the beloved community amid outer turmoil. That noble, necessary, and hard but achievable vision beckons us today more than ever in a world teetering on the brink of nuclear suicide and spiritual insanity desperately hungering for moral leadership. Our leaders continue to talk about peace while spending trillions preparing for and waging war. Poverty, hunger, and sickness still ravish the bodies, minds, and spirits of millions of children in our materially rich but morally stunted nation and world. Countless children have been deprived of childhood's innocence, trust, and hopefulness wondering whether they will grow up in developing countries, in our inner-city war zones, and suburban enclaves where a seventeen-year-old asks: "How are we supposed to start our lives with death looking over our shoulders?" After 9/11, a ten-year-old from Connecticut said: "I'll never trust the sky again."

The *Bulletin of the Atomic Scientists* has moved its Doomsday Clock back and forth since 1968, when it was set at seven minutes before midnight. Today it stands at five minutes to midnight as more nations possess nuclear weapons with the scary possibility they could fall into the hands of rogue nations and terrorists. Equally disturbing is the grim reality that the United States and Russia, despite the thaw in relationship, still maintain more than ten thousand nuclear warheads poised to kill every person in our two countries in a few minutes. Rhetoric about producing more "effective" nuclear weapons makes not a sliver of sense. How could we stop the world spiraling out of control if any nation dared unleash a nuclear weapon ever again to win any war for any reason? Who are the maniacs who even consider putting a nuclear option on the table in today's world? Have they forgotten that "the earth is the Lord's and the fullness thereof and all they that dwell therein"? Who made them God?

Martin, how did we reach this insane place? Is this any way to thank our Creator for the life and Earth lent us in trust for all generations to come? Is the cloud of potential destruction of human life the legacy we want to bequeath to our children and grandchildren? Has our scientific technology simply enabled us to go backward faster? How do we extricate our children and grandchildren from this nuclear prison? As the world's leader in military expenditures and exports and nuclear capability, can America become the leader in nuclear disarmament, rather than nuclear armament, and pull us back from the edge of human extinction? National nuclear supremacy or winning a war with nuclear weapons mean nothing in a nonexistent world!

I don't want my children and grandchildren growing up under this shadow of man's ultimate evil hand. Nor do I want any child anywhere in our world being unable to grow up, or growing up embittered, because unused weapons of any kind are robbing them of food, health care, education, clean water, jobs, and the respect and protection owed them as children of God. I want to leave future generations a world of friends not enemies.

Thankfully, former vice president Al Gore has become our environmental Paul Revere warning the world about the dangers of global warming and the degradation of Mother Earth. Although our nation constitutes 5 percent of the world's population, we consume more than a quarter of the world's energy, and our eyes are still opening too slowly to the folly of engaging in more wars to support our addictions to oil and consumption and we are failing to adequately develop alternative and safer sources of energy. Sadly, your warnings about the dangers of excessive materialism and militarism are going largely unheeded. Since you died with the Vietnam War raging, we have been engaged in ten military actions, including the current wars in Iraq and Afghanistan, and have spent more than $16 trillion on the military.

You warned not only about militarism but about the dangers of poverty and greed—both obscenely rampant today. The net worth of the world's 946 billionaires, most Americans, exceeds the combined gross domestic product of 138 countries with a combined population of nearly 2 billion people. How can we achieve a stable world when so few have so much and so many have so little? You said something was wrong with capitalism as it is practiced in the United States. Recently released IRS data on America's four hundred highest income taxpayers in 2005 confirmed just how right you were. *The Wall Street Journal* and the Center on Budget and Policy Priorities analyses report the income of these few skyrocketed between 1992 and 2005 to an average adjusted gross income of $214 million and combined income of almost $86 billion. But after capital gains tax cuts in 1997 and 2003, they saw a drop in their taxes of $25 million per filer in

2005 or a total of $10 billion in tax reductions! This staggering one-year tax cut to just these four hundred richest Americans could have provided more than 7 million uninsured children health coverage for a year, which Congress and President Bush said we could not afford. The Associated Press reported that one American earned $5.13 billion in compensation and stock in 2007. That's $427 million a month; $99 million a week; $14 million a day; $585,600 an hour! He made more in an hour than twelve elementary school teachers make in a year. In 2006, one oil company executive earned $322 million, equivalent to the average annual salaries of more than 12,400 preschool teachers ($25,900).

Incredibly, many of the richest and most powerful among us still don't seem to recognize that enough is enough as our economy hovers on the edge of recession and as millions more children have fallen into poverty and lost health insurance.

In 2005 Hurricane Katrina ripped away the thin false veil of shared prosperity and revealed the pervasive poverty suffered by hundreds of thousands of families in Louisiana and Mississippi. They were left behind as the water washed away the poorly constructed levees of New Orleans because they had no way out. Ill-prepared city, state, and federal governments responded with incredible incompetence and indifference, although many Americans poured their hearts out to help. Yet three years later, tens of thousands of Katrina's children and other survivors are still waiting for their government to rescue them from homelessness, unspeakable poverty, dysfunctional public schools and health and mental health systems, and post-traumatic stress disorders. And while the suffering of the poor persists and is growing not only in Louisiana and Mississippi but all across America with increasing food insecurity, credit card bankruptcies, and home and job losses, many of our leaders want to make the obscene tax cuts for the top I percent permanent and even falsely call their expiration a tax increase. Who in the world taught such reckless disregard for the common good? Why do we Americans tolerate public and private sector leaders who engage in such overreaching?

If our nation's riches were shared more fairly among all Americans, and the rich got richer at a slower rate through a fairer tax structure and fewer government subsidies for powerful special interests and individuals and more tax relief and subsidies for low- and moderate-income families, millions of children could escape poverty and get the basic necessities they need now to grow up to be healthy and educated adults.

I hope a critical mass of citizens and political leaders in both parties will stand up and demand that the massive tax cuts for at least the top I percent of the richest Americans will be allowed to expire, insist on closing huge corporate loopholes that result in gigantic companies reporting tens of billions of profits paying no taxes, and stop rewarding corporations with tax breaks for sending jobs abroad.

What we have experienced over the last eight years, is nothing less than an ideological and economic coup d'etat. While America slept, and those who should and could speak up remained silent, a majority of our political leaders, in both parties, with the acquiescence of most of America's media, stood by as our president and congressional leaders robbed the public purse through profligate tax cuts for people and special interests who did not need them; wiped out our budget surplus and dug us further into debt, averaging more than $17,000 per person, with the majority of the burden falling on our children; mortgaged our nation to competitor nations like China to pay our mounting bills; and entered two costly wars with no end in sight.

The greatest sin of these ill-conceived tax cuts and wars, each of which costs trillions of dollars, is that they have stolen from our children and the poor, not just in our own nation but in the world, where we had the opportunity to invest in their lives and show them an America that cares. Why can't the greedy find a way to ensure a minimal safety net for human beings while earning generous, rather than grossly excessive profits? You repeatedly told us that we will preempt violence only by replacing despair with hope. Hope is food and shelter and work and education and health care. Nothing short of a massive, nonviolent, cross-racial and cross-income movement to remove from office and leadership people who have taken from the weak to give to the powerful will be able to curb the runaway hubris of a few risking the physical and economic survival and security of all of us.

Where are the voices like yours calling for common and moral sense today? Where are the leaders and citizens willing to struggle together to stem the out of control militarism, private-sector greed, and materialism that still drives us, to close the unprecedented gap between rich and poor, and to end the poverty and downward mobility of large numbers of our children? I'm confident that if you were here today you would say ending poverty is the top domestic and world concern facing us and would be calling for another Poor People's Campaign.

Eradicating child poverty as a down payment on ending poverty for all will enable millions of children left behind to enter life on a more even playing field and reach the first base of life in first grade ready to learn, rather than already pronounced failures, if we invest in cost-effective health, quality early childhood and parent supports for them. They will be able to make it to the second base in life if all schools provide all our children a quality education. We cannot wait another minute to correct the *massive* failure of our current largely segregated and still unequal public education system in which 85 percent of low-income public school eighth graders cannot read or do math at grade level. Since children spend only 17 percent of their time in school and 83 percent out of school over the course of a year, investing in high-quality after school and summer enrichment programs and utilizing summer feeding programs to stave off hunger will help more children get to third base. Young people need to see and believe they can reach home plate if they stay in school and that a decent job and a chance to go to college are real. And the playing field our children grow up on must be cleared of the guns, drugs, and cultural pollution that kill and lead so many astray. We must fill the ballpark's bleachers with positive adult cheerleaders—parents; teachers; neighbors; and religious, community, political, and cultural leaders—beckoning and cheering them on to success, and comforting and sticking with them when they strike out or lose games along the way. And we need to make sure they have skilled coaches and ample baseballs and bats to help them play the game of life well and win.

In some deep hidden crevice of my heart, your assassination seemed almost inevitable. Nonetheless, when it happened April 4, I—like millions of others—was devastated and completely overcome with a profound sense of personal and collective loss.

The violence you tried to prevent all your life erupted in riots of rage and despair in inner cities all over America, including Washington, D.C. Robert Kennedy, campaigning for president in Indianapolis, hearing of your slaying, immediately went to speak to inner-city black citizens, reminding them that a white man's gun had taken his brother's life and that "what we need in the United States is not violence; what we need in the United States is not hatred; what we need in the United States is not violence or lawlessness; but love and wisdom and compassion toward one another, and a feeling of justice toward those who still suffer within our country, whether they be white or they be black. . . . Let us dedicate ourselves to what the Greeks wrote so many years ago: 'to tame the savageness of man and make gentle the life of this world.' "

You always called riots "the language of the unheard," and now our voice of conscience—your voice—was silenced. Eleven days later Robert Kennedy spoke movingly again about the "senseless menace of violence." "No one—no matter where he lives or what he does—can be certain who will suffer from some senseless bloodshed. And yet it goes on and on and on in this country of ours." Two months later, on June 6, my birthday, he died from an assassin's bullet in Los Angeles after winning the California Democratic primary.

Our country did not listen to either of you. Since your assassinations in 1968, *more than 1.2 million* men, women, and children have been killed by firearms and another 750,000 have died violently by other means in our nation's relentless undeclared civil war. This death toll of nearly 2 million human beings in our nation is nearly four times the number of American battle deaths reported in all the wars of the twentieth and twenty-first centuries.

Most shamefully, since 1979, more than 104,000 American children and teens have been killed. This equals 4,177 classrooms of twenty-five children and is over twice the combined American battle casualty toll in Vietnam, Iraq, and Afghanistan of 51,130 as of April 5, 2008. Another 500,000 children and teens have been wounded. CDF's most recent annual child gun violence report found 3,006 children died from gunfire in 2005—eight a day; fifty-eight a week. We've made progress: It was sixteen a day when we began our anti–gun violence campaign after many black youth told us they did not think they would live to adulthood. Every four days, we lose as many children from gunfire as died in the massacre of 32 people at Virginia Tech in April 2007. And it goes on and on.

Where are the books and media coverage of our chronic internal war that has no end in sight? Where is everyone? Why don't we care? Why don't we say **STOP!** Why don't we speak up and organize more effectively to break the National Rifle Association (NRA) lock on national gun policy, which ignores the overwhelming majority of citizens' desire for commonsense gun control?

The day after your assassination in 1968, I went out into the riot-torn streets of Washington, D.C., and into schools in neighborhoods scorched by flames to talk to children. I told them not to be violent or loot and raid so that they would not get arrested and ruin their futures. A young black boy, about twelve or thirteen years old, looked me squarely in the eyes and said, "Lady, what future? I ain't got no future. I ain't got nothing to lose." I've spent the four decades since you left us, and will spend the rest of my life, trying to prove him wrong in our powerful and wealthy nation. *I had no idea how hard it would be.* For this child saw and spoke the plain truth for himself and millions like him in our economically and militarily powerful but spiritually anemic society.

I am *so* worried that the racial progress of the last half century that you and countless others sacrificed to achieve is imperiled by increasing incarceration, which is creating a new American apartheid. States are spending on average almost three times as much per prisoner as per public school pupil and in some states the increase in prison spending exceeds the increase in higher education spending. America has become the world's leading jailer, with one in a hundred Americans behind bars and 7.2 million people in prison, jail, on parole, or on probation. Political, community, faith, black, and Latino leaders in every sector must mobilize to stop the growing and racially inequitable incarceration of our parents and children, a majority for nonviolent offenses. The Pew Center on the States reports that one in nine black men and one in thirty-six Hispanic men aged twenty to thirty-four are serving time and that black men are twelve times as likely as white men to be imprisoned for drug offenses despite almost equal rates of illegal drug use. Prisons are becoming big business.

This imprisonment of America is an all-hands-on-deck crisis if we are to reroute our children from the prison pipeline to healthy adulthood by reweaving the fabric of family and community and demanding just public policies and practices focused on prevention and early intervention rather than punishment as a first resort. We so miss your strong voice and are saddened that many leaders of color don't take any better care of poor children and youth than white leaders who neglect them. Many of the cities and counties with the largest numbers of poor children being fed into the prison pipeline have mayors and supervisors of color. Many of the school districts where poor children are being provided an abysmal education and are being subjected to inappropriate zero tolerance school discipline policies have superintendents and school board members of color. We need servant leaders of all colors—not self-serving leaders—if we are to build strong communities and save our children and future.

GREAT RACIAL PROGRESS AND HOPE

AMID CONTINUING PERIL IN AMERICA

In a nation-defining election year, we are reaching toward a more united America. Our centuries-old impenetrable glass ceilings of race and gender have been pierced and America's political DNA has stretched to mirror the more than half of our human race that is female and the two-thirds that is nonwhite with an African-American and a woman as leading contenders for the Democratic nomination for president in 2008. We have not seen the youth so politically engaged since 1968.

There is much other racial progress to report in addition to the momentous victory of Barack Obama as the Democratic standard-bearer for president. In 1968, there were fewer than 1,500 black elected officials; today there are more than 9,500, including 43 members of the Congressional Black Caucus; 14 black mayors of cities with populations over 50,000; and 43 black and 6 Latino statewide elected officials. Thurgood Marshall was our first black U.S. Supreme Court Justice and Clarence Thomas is our second (a symbol rather than a vessel of progress, a too prevalent occurrence over the last decades, as many talented blacks donned the cloaks of leaders espousing militaristic policies and those that increase the racial and income divides). Seven blacks and 4 Latinos head Fortune 500 companies. In 2008, two blacks serve in the president's cabinet and fourteen black astronauts have explored space. Seven blacks have been awarded Nobel Prizes and countless others excel in literature, economics, science, and in striving for a more peaceful world. In 2006, black purchasing power was almost $650 billion—four times that of 1968, equivalent to the combined

GDP of Israel, Egypt, Hungary, New Zealand, Singapore, and Vietnam and more than the GDP of Sweden, Switzerland, and Belgium. Thousands of young people of color attend college and have become doctors, dentists, lawyers, and judges. When I went to practice law in Mississippi in 1964, there were only four black lawyers for 900,000 black citizens and the three who took civil rights cases had never gone to law school. Today, there are more than four hundred and two of my former law clerks who served as Mississippi Supreme Court Justices are now senior partners in leading Jackson law firms.

These major strides by a significant minority of people of color—and women—into the corridors of power and mainstream American society have not extended to millions of poor blacks, Latinos, Native Americans, and whites who are increasingly being left behind in our rich nation. Not only are there still two Americas there are two black Americas with a significant minority doing well but a majority treading water or living near or in poverty, even extreme poverty. Many of our children will not do as well as their parents' generation. This is particularly true for African Americans where nearly a third will do less well than their parents.

The drain of successful black role models from previously segregated communities has robbed many black children and youth of a sense of the possible and a positive vision of the future.

The black community must reclaim our traditional values of family, community, and self-help, regain and share with all our children—and with all in America—the spiritual legacy of the black struggle for justice, and catalyze and mount a powerful crusade to save all our children, joining with our Latino brothers and sisters and all people who share your goals of a beloved community. We must train a critical mass of young servant-leaders to take up your torch—armed with nonviolence and the skills needed to build the twenty-first-century movement in much more complex terrain and galvanize the dormant but powerful voices of women of all races. The faith community must remember the God they profess to serve and stop being cultural puppets. And we must continue to struggle against the resegregation of American society by race, income, gender, and incarceration that undermine the realization of a united nation blessed with a rich diversity of people. Integration, as you believed, does not mean losing who you are; it is sharing who you are, forging mutually respectful and equal relationships with others.

You blessed America with your rich faith, spiritual traditions, and prophetic preaching. You gave us your deep and abiding love and lifelong commitment to nonviolence. You shared your moral clarity and courageous truth telling. You left us your unrelenting commitment to justice for the poor and every one of God's children. You showed us the way through your example and call for massive nonviolent action in the service of justice and peace. And you gave us your life.

Thank you. We will carry on.

A Letter to God: Prayers for Our Children, Country, and World

I believe that only prayer from the heart and in action will save our nation and world. These prayers seek God's guidance and help in the struggle to save children and get our nation and world on a safer and more just course. Our neglect and abuse of children is a profound spiritual crisis requiring transformation of the heart.

O GOD OF ALL CHILDREN

O God of the children of Sarajevo, Somalia, South Africa, and South
    Carolina,
Of Afghanistan, Pakistan, and India, Iraq, Iran, and Israel
Of Cairo, the Congo and Chicago, Darfur and Detroit
Of Myanmar and Mississippi, Louisiana and Yemen
Help us to love and respect and protect them all.

O God of black and brown and white and albino children and those
    all mixed together,

Of children who are rich and poor and in between,
Of children who speak English and Russian and Hmong and Spanish
   and Chinese and languages our ears cannot discern,
Help us to love and respect and protect them all.

O God of the child prodigy and the child prostitute, of the child of
   rapture and the child of rape.
Of runaway or thrown away children who struggle every day without
   parent or place or friend or future,
Help us to love and respect and protect them all.

O God of children who can walk and talk and hear and see and sing
   and dance and jump and play and of children who wish they could
   but can't
Of children who are loved and unloved, wanted and unwanted,
Help us to love and respect and protect them all.

O God of beggar; beaten; abused; neglected; homeless; and AIDS-,
   drug-, violence-, and hunger-ravaged children,
Of children who are emotionally and physically and mentally fragile,
   and of children who rebel and ridicule, torment and taunt,
Help us to love and respect and protect them all.

O God of children of destiny and of despair, of war and of peace,
Of disfigured, diseased, and dying children,
Of children without hope and of children with hope to spare and to
   share,
Help us to love and respect and protect them all.

GOD PLEASE FORGIVE AND TRANSFORM OUR
RICH NATION AND WORLD

O God, please forgive and transform our rich nation and world, where small babies die of hunger and homelessness quite legally.

O God, please forgive and transform our rich nation and world, where infants and school children die from guns sold quite legally.

O God, please forgive and transform our rich nation and world, where the rich continue to get more at the expense of the poor quite legally.

O God, please forgive and transform our rich nation and world, which thinks security rests in missiles rather than in mothers, and in bombs rather than babies.

O God, please forgive and transform our rich nation and world, which thinks our strength rests in ourselves rather than in You and in military might rather than in moral right.

O God, please forgive and transform our rich nation and world, for not giving You sufficient thanks by sharing with others their daily bread.

O God, please help us to repent and to stop confusing what is quite legal with what is just and right in Your sight.

Please grant us Your vision in Your time for our children's sake.

GOD HELP US TO END POVERTY IN OUR TIME

God help us to end poverty in our time.

The poverty of having a child with too little to eat and no place to sleep, no air, sunlight and space to breathe, bask, and grow.

The poverty of watching your child suffer and get sicker and sicker and not knowing what to do or how to get help because you don't have a car or health insurance.

The poverty of working your fingers to the bone every day taking care of somebody else's children and neglecting your own, and still not being able to pay your bills.

The poverty of having a job that does not let you afford a stable place to live and being terrified you'll become homeless and lose your children to foster care.

The poverty of losing your job because you cannot find reliable child care or transportation to work.

The poverty of working all your life caring for others and having to start all over again caring for the grandchildren you love.

The poverty of earning a college degree, having children, opening a day care center, and taking home $300 a week or month if you're lucky.

The poverty of loneliness and isolation and alienation—having no one to call or visit, tell you where to get help, assist you in getting it, or care if you're living or dead.

The poverty of having too much and sharing too little and having the burden of nothing to carry.

The poverty of convenient blindness and deafness and indifference to others, of emptiness and enslavement to things, drugs, power, violence, and fleeting fame.

The poverty of low aim and paltry purpose, weak will and tiny vision, big meetings and small action, loud talk and sullen grudging service.

The poverty of believing in nothing, standing for nothing, sharing nothing, sacrificing nothing, struggling for nothing.

The poverty of pride and ingratitude for God's gifts of life and children and family and freedom and country and not wanting for others what you want for yourself.

The poverty of greed for more and more and more, ignoring, blaming, and exploiting the needy, and taking from the weak to please the strong.

The poverty of addiction to drugs, to drink, to work, to self, to the
status quo, and to injustice.

The poverty of fear that keeps you from doing the thing you think is
right.

The poverty of despair and cynicism.

God help us end poverty in our time in all its faces and places, young
and old, rural, urban, suburban and small town too, and in every
color of humans You have made everywhere.

God help us to end poverty in our time in all its guises—inside and
out—physical and spiritual, so that all our and Your children may
live the lives that you intend.

A COVENANT TO PRAY AND STAND FOR CHILDREN

We *will* pray and stand for children blessed by parents who care and
for children without a parent or anyone who cares at all.

We *will* pray and stand for children filled with joy and for children
whose days and nights are joyless.

We *will* pray and stand for children with hope and for children whose
spirits have been dimmed and dashed.

We *will* pray and stand for children high on play and study and
laughter and for children high on pot, glue, cocaine, and ecstasy.

We *will* pray and stand for children for whom we pray every day and
for children who have no one to pray for them along life's way.

We *will* pray and stand for children poised by circumstance to soar and
conquer life's challenges and for children bogged down by the pain
of survival.

We *will* pray and stand for children who love to read and for children who can't read at all, for children who learn with excitement and for children told by adults that they cannot achieve.

We *will* pray and stand for children who expect and are helped to succeed and for children whom no one believes in or helps to succeed.

We *will* pray that we will be a help and not a hindrance to children we call our own and to children You created who are part of our family too.

A CHILD ADVOCATE'S BEATITUDES
(INSPIRED BY CLARENCE JORDAN'S *Sermon on the Mount*)

Blessed are the poor in spirit—who do not measure themselves by money or worldly power but who ask God for what they need and are not mired in pride—for theirs is the kingdom of God.

Blessed are those who mourn—who are concerned about the needs of children and the poor and others in need who cannot speak for themselves—for they will be comforted.

Blessed are the meek—who do not seek only their own good but their neighbors' too—for they will inherit the earth.

Blessed are those who hunger and thirst after righteousness—who do not work for the praise of others or earthly gain or fame and share gladly their talents, energy, and money—for they will be filled.

Blessed are the merciful—who know they are sinners and are dependent on God's and others' forgiveness every minute of every day—for they will receive mercy.

Blessed are the pure in heart—who are not hypocrites but who struggle to live what they preach—for they will see God.

Blessed are the peacemakers—who do not prepare for war while talking about peace, who do not kill others in order to stop killing, who do not love just those who love them but reach out to make their enemies friends—for they will be called children of God.

Blessed are those who are persecuted for righteousness' sake—who do not run or waver in the face of criticism, threats, or death—for theirs is the kingdom of heaven.

Blessed are those who speak kindly and not meanly of others—who do not tear down others but build them up for the kingdom's work and children's well-being—for they shall receive their reward.

Blessed are the just—who do not adhere to the letter of the law and regulations for some but ignore them for others—for they will hear God's well done.

LET ALL THE LITTLE CHILDREN COME

Let the little children come unto me and forbid them not, for such is the kingdom of heaven, Jesus said.

He did not say let only rich or middle-class white children come.

He did not say let only the strapping boys but not the girls come.

He did not say let only the able-bodied children come.

All the children He bade come.

He did not say let all my children or your children or our friends' children or those in our families and neighborhoods and who look and act and speak like us come.

He did not say let only the well-behaved nice children come or those who conform to society's norms.

He did not say let a few, a third, half, or three fourths come—but *all*.

Jesus said let the little children come and forbid them not, for such is the kingdom of heaven.

A PLEA THAT OUR EYES, EARS, AND HEARTS
MAY BE OPENED

Open our eyes that we may see the need all around us.

Open our ears that we may hear the cries of Your children for food
and shelter and relief from sickness and danger.

Open our minds that we may understand and live Your word and will
in our lives.

Open our hearts so that we may radiate Your loving spirit in all
we do.

A PRAYER FOR THOSE WITH NO ONE TO PRAY FOR THEM

O God, I pray for those who have no one to pray for and protect them.
For the homeless addicts I have passed on the street today; for the
child being sexually assaulted and physically and emotionally
abused right now; for the mothers dying every minute somewhere
in our world and whose children are stillborn or will die in the
first days of life. Hear our prayer and guide our feet and lift our
cries around the world to stop the senseless deaths of mothers and
children everywhere.

GOD BLESS AMERICA

God bless America to live her creed in deed and to reach out to all
those in need at home and in all Your world.

God bless America to be a blessing to the nations of the world spread-
ing freedom and justice by example, respect, and help.

God bless America to heed Your prophets' calls for justice for the weak, the oppressed, orphans, widows, and strangers.

God bless America to protect the futures of all our world's children and to pass on to them a better and safer earth where all may dwell in peace.

Resource List

Jonah Edelman
Stand for Children
516 SE Morrison Street,
Suite 410
Portland, OR 97214
Phone: 800-663-4032
Fax: 503-963-9517
www.stand.org
stand@stand.org

Geoffrey Canada
Harlem Children's Zone
35 East 125th Street
New York, NY 10035
Phone: 212-360-3255
Fax: 212-289-0661
TTY: 1-800-662-1220
www.hcz.org
mlipp@harlemchildrenszone.org

Pastor Ray Hammond
Boston Ten Point Coalition
215 Forest Hills Street
Boston, MA 02130
Phone: 617-524-4331
Fax: 617-524-4962
www.bostontenpoint.org

Michael Evans
Wake County School System
3600 Wake Forest Road
P.O. Box 28041
Raleigh, NC 27611-8041
Phone: 919-850-1700
www.wcpss.net
mrevans@wcpss.net

Children's Defense Fund
25 E Street, NW
Washington, DC 20001
Phone: 202-628-8787
www.childrensdefense.org